IF SHE
IS RAPED

Alan W. McEvoy and Jeff B. Brookings

LP **Learning Publications, Inc.**
HOLMES BEACH, FL   MONTREAL

Learning Publications, Inc.
5351 Gulf Drive
P. O. Box 1338
Holmes Beach, FL 34218-1338

Printed in the United States of America

Printing: 5 4 3   Year: 5

ISBN: 1-55691-062-2

With love to Allison, Cindy, Katy, Kyle, Ellie, Riley, and Sarah.

CONTENTS

PREFACE

If your wife, daughter, or woman friend is raped, this book will give you practical ways to help her recover. You will learn to understand what happens to her in the aftermath of sexual assault. You will learn what you should and should not do. You will learn how to deal with the legal system if the rape is reported. Finally, this book will help you to deal with your own feelings, and it will give you the tools necessary to maintain a healthy relationship with the person you love.

ACKNOWLEDGEMENTS

We wish to express our deep appreciation to the staff of Project Woman for their kind cooperation. Special thanks are also due to Harold Nordeman, Sally Scheuerman and Vicki Ziegenhagen for their assistance. Finally, we wish to thank all those who work with rape victims and their families; it is to these helpers that this book is dedicated.

1
Understanding Rape

Forcible rape is an act of sexual violence which is usually accompanied by physical threat, and which is nearly always done to females by males. Rape and attempted rape are disturbingly frequent crimes, occurring tens of thousands of times each year in the United States and Canada. For example, the FBI's Uniform Crime Reports confirmed over 92,000 rapes in 1988. Since sexual assault so often goes unreported, most experts agree that these statistics are at best a very conservative estimate.

In recent years, rape has become the topic of numerous research studies, newspaper stories, and television documentaries. The women's movement in particular has focused attention on the traumatic nature of rape, the reasons for such acts of violence against women, and the role of the criminal justice system. As a result, public awareness concerning the seriousness of rape has been enhanced, the criminal justice system has begun to deal with rape as more than just a minor crime, and hundreds of rape crisis centers have been established to assist victims.

As might be expected, most of the resources of rape crisis centers, investigative units in police departments and counseling facilities are directed toward providing immediate assistance to the victim. However, rape is a crime that deeply affects not only the woman, but also family members and other loved ones. Because of the violent and sexual nature of rape, men who are important to the victim—the husbands, fathers and male friends—usually have a particularly difficult time coming to terms with what has happened to her.

Yet these males often have the greatest impact on her recovery. This impact may be positive or negative, depending upon what they say and do. By understanding the true nature and consequences of rape, however, men can play a crucial role in helping her deal with the short-term and long-term consequences of this traumatic life event.

Although most males will want to help their loved ones if they are sexually assaulted, many are ill-prepared to respond constructively. Many of them think of rape as only a "woman's problem." They have little awareness of how rape can impact on their relationships. To make matters worse, prevailing cultural myths result in other misunderstandings about rape. These misunderstandings greatly compound the difficulties of a victim's recovery. In summary, many males are well-intentioned but simply do not know what to do, or worse, they respond poorly to the recovery needs of the women they love.

FACTS AND MYTHS ABOUT RAPE

There is no such thing as a "typical" rape or rape victim. Each episode represents a unique and terrifying experience. However, there are a number of common elements and misconceptions associated with rape; awareness of them will help sensitize you to what she has been through.

To begin, we cannot overstate the point that rape is not the same as "making love." Although the majority of completed rapes involve vaginal penetration, this occurs in a state of emotional terror without the woman giving consent. It is a complete misconception to believe that women "secretly desire" to be raped or taken by force. Rape is a total violation of a woman's rights over her own body and of her ability to make a sexual choice. Indeed, from the woman's point of view, the sexual dimension of rape often assumes lesser importance than the violent aspects.

Rape is fundamentally an act of violence. Many rapes involve threats of bodily harm and often the woman suffers severe physical injury. Threats of violence are made even worse by the presence of a weapon and intimidating verbal abuse. Any implication that the woman "asked for" or enjoyed the experience, or that rape and making love are the same, is a basic misconception. Even in the context of a dating relationship—a situation where large numbers of rapes occur—the rape still represents a violent assault and not something which the victim wants or enjoys. It is never appropriate to suggest that a woman somehow benefits from being the target of a sexual assault.

A related fact is that the woman is absolutely not responsible for her victimization. Men often mistakenly assume that victims could prevent rape by avoiding certain social situations, by dressing differently, or by putting up a fight. This mistaken assumption may be even greater if the victim exhibits no visible physical injuries. Some males incorrectly believe that if she didn't actively resist the attack, she must have given tacit consent. Such a belief suggests that the victim is responsible for the assault. The truth is that virtually anyone placed in a life-threatening situation can be paralyzed by fear or recognize the futility of physical resistance.

Furthermore, rape occurs at all hours of the day or night and in virtually any setting, including one's own home or a public place. Believing that she is partially responsible only places emotional distance between the two of you at a time when your support is most needed. This causes unnecessary feelings of guilt, anger and isolation. Ultimately, blaming her prolongs her recovery and adds great strain to your relationship with her.

Finally, it is important to realize that rape can happen to anyone, regardless of age, income, appearance or personal reputation. It is true that the majority of rape victims are single women between the ages of twelve and twenty-four. However, there is no way to predict which women are likely to be selected as victims. The one common element is that rape is a frightening and degrading experience; victims require a period of time to recover. Furthermore, we know that men also are affected deeply by the rape of a loved one, that men can learn to understand her victimization, and that they can and often do act in a manner contributing to her recovery.

HOW YOU CAN HELP

You can help her by:

- **knowing** what to expect from her and others following the rape;

- **recognizing and accepting** her feelings, as well as your own and others close to her;

- **communicating** to her a sense of compassion and acceptance;

- **allowing** her to make decisions which help her to regain control over her life; and

● **sharing** with her so that she senses she is not alone, that she has your unconditional love and support, and that this is a crisis you will endure together.

Remember, rape is a violent crime that is neither sought nor caused by the victim. Helping her to recover should be your chief concern.

2
Addressing Immediate Concerns

The period immediately following a rape is an emotionally charged, confusing, and extremely anxious time. Not only has she been terrorized and totally violated, but she now is faced with many additional worries. For example, directly following the rape, victims typically consider such questions as:

"Do I need medical attention?"

"Do I report this to the police?"

"Am I pregnant?"

"Did I contract venereal disease or AIDS?"

"Should I tell my family?"

"What will others think of me?"

"How will this affect those I love?"

"Will he attempt to rape me again?"

"Will my life ever return to normal?"

Obviously, the emotional consequences of rape continue well beyond the event. Unfortunately, doctors, police and lawyers often unintentionally contribute to her trauma as they carry out their bureaucratic routines in hospitals and police departments. For example, if the victim decides to immediately report the rape to the police, she is required to undergo a series of medical exams—for legal reasons—*before* she has the opportunity to bathe and change clothing.   This may entail a lengthy wait in a hospital emergency room followed by a series of medical examinations.

In the process of providing evidence to the police, she may have to recount the rape several times in detail to strangers (usually men). She may be required to examine "mug" shots or help construct composite sketches of the rapist if his identity is not known to her. In some cases, police ask the victim to submit to a polygraph exam. Unfortunately, a police request to take a "lie detector test" unintentionally communicates the message that the police do not believe her report of being raped. Similarly, they may not take her story seriously if the test results are ambiguous.

The victim has every right to refuse to take a polygraph test and still expect her reported assault to be taken seriously. Lie detectors should not be used to determine a rape victim's credibility. Fortunately, most police investigators recognize this and seek to obtain evidence from the victim by other means. However, she may also request to take the test in order to further establish the credibility of her story.

While it is true that rules of evidence require detailed questioning by police, the examination procedures may appear to her as both unnecessary and as an invasion of privacy. At the very moment she most needs sympathetic understanding, impersonal routines can add to an already heavy emotional burden.

Even if she chooses not to call the police, she still should be examined by a physician. First, she may require immediate medical attention. In addition, if she changes her mind and decides to report the rape, she will need medical evidence to take legal action. Finally, because some tests do not yield immediate results, she will need to return to the physician approximately three weeks after the rape to take these tests.

Assisting her in receiving medical attention conveys the message that you believe her account and that you view her assault seriously. You are therefore communicating a powerful message of concern and support by letting her know that you are in this together and that this is not something she must face alone.

The period of time immediately following the rape requires great care because the psychological forces contributing to her recovery are set in motion. How and what you communicate to her are critical in determining how she interprets the rape incident and how she feels about herself. In order to help her, there are a number of things you should and should not do.

HOW YOU SHOULD RESPOND

- The most common initial reaction among men is an intense anger and a strong desire to seek revenge against the rapist. This is normal and understandable. However, this is a time when calm and reasoned judgments are most needed. It is especially important that you do not personally contact the rapist, even if his identity is known to you. Contact can create legal problems for you and place the woman in the position of having to deal with additional fears concerning your safety. Threatening to take the law into your own hands only adds unnecessarily to her emotional burden.

- Making threats against the rapist is undesirable for other reasons as well. Your anger and threats of revenge shift attention away from her needs to you. At a time when she most needs nurturance and understanding, the focus becomes your anger rather than her recovery needs. Moreover, your anger can cut off communication; she may feel unable to talk about the incident because she does not wish to upset you. She may even feel guilty for "imposing" such an emotional burden on you. Finally, threatening revenge may cause her to fear you because your feelings of rage add a measure of unpredictability to the relationship. Letting your anger dominate only closes the lines of communication and reduces her sense of stability.

- Under no circumstances should you accuse her or judge her. It is important for you to remain calm and to give her the opportunity, if she desires, to discuss the experience. The thing she may want and need most is simply to be held and spoken to with gentleness.

- Tell her that she is not responsible for being raped. Do not ask her questions like "Why didn't you scream and run? Why were you at that place at that time? Why did you talk to him in the first place?" Such "why" questions as these convey a sense of being judgmental, and may make her feel guilty and possibly even resentful toward you. She needs to know that you do not blame her for failing to resist the rapist or for being in a situation that resulted in rape.

- You absolutely should avoid suggesting that she secretly may have enjoyed the experience. Rape is a violent act that is not a source of pleasure for the victim. It is important for her to feel reassured that you do not equate her rape with an act of infidelity or promiscuity, and that you do not see her as defiled or less moral than prior to the incident.

- Just as many males accept as true some of the myths and stereotypes about rape, so too do many women. When she is ready, encourage her to discuss any beliefs about rape which may contribute to her emotional state. Convince her that you do not share those views which place the woman at fault. It is especially important for you to let her know that you believe her, even though others may have doubts. Doubting her version of events undermines her ability to share feelings with you.

- Sexual assault robs the woman of a sense of control over her life. In order for her to regain this sense of control, she should be encouraged to

make decisions about all events affecting her life
(e.g., whether to report the crime, go to trial, tell
family and friends, seek counseling, etc.). Do not
attempt to make these decisions for her or
demand that she follow a particular course of
action, even though you want to help her by
"taking charge." It is important for you to
communicate your unfailing support for her in
whatever decisions she makes. By playing a more
supportive role, you are putting her in the position
of again assuming control over her life.

- Don't demand of her immediate, open
  communication about the rape. She may not have
  had sufficient time to sort out her feelings, or she
  may wish to guard her feelings due to a
  deep-seated sense of embarrassment. It is
  particularly important that you refrain from
  unintentionally humiliating her by prying into the
  sexually intimate aspects of the rape. Accept the
  fact that she will discuss her feelings when she is
  ready.

Remember, she needs to feel that she is not alone and
that you will endure this crisis together. Regardless of what
happened, she should know that your love and support
remain intact.

3
Communicating with the Victim

For the rape victim, having to relate the incident to you and to other significant persons in her life can be a major source of anxiety. Effective communication is very important to her long-term adjustment and to the survival of her valued relationships. Unfortunately, a large percentage of these relationships end or undergo severe strain in the aftermath of an assault. The primary reason for this is that the system of communication between the victim and others tends to break down.

WHAT TO SAY TO THE VICTIM

Given the emotional turmoil you both are experiencing, there are several steps you can take to promote effective communication.

- Be a patient and approachable listener. This requires sensitivity to her feelings and a willingness to demonstrate unconditional acceptance. By giving her the opportunity to express feelings when she is ready, you will help her work through emotional conflicts and you will gain a better understanding of her needs.

- Don't pressure or "interrogate" by insisting that she recount the details of the incident over and over again. When she is ready to discuss the rape and her feelings about it, she will do so. Forcing her to be candid intensifies her confusion and may make her resent you.

- You should never express anger toward her if she initially is reluctant to talk, or if she delays telling you for a period of time. Do not accuse her of "hiding something" because she did not tell you sooner. She may wish to protect loved ones from the pain and turmoil caused by the revelation of being raped. She may also fear being blamed or rejected. Her remaining silent should not be interpreted as a rejection of you, but as her way of sorting things out.

- Pay special attention to recurring themes in her conversations. These might be clues providing insight into issues which are especially troublesome to her. Being raped can bring out much "unfinished business" that has long troubled her, including problems which may already exist in her relationship with you. By being alert to her conversational themes and by being open to discuss sensitive issues, you will come to better understand her emotional state and help her to resolve problems.

- Eventually, it is important for the two of you to discuss the impact of the rape on your relationship. The emotional consequences of rape are traumatic for all those involved in a personal relationship with the woman, especially you. Calmly sharing your feelings and vulnerabilities with her affords her the opportunity to nurture you, just as you have been nurturing her. Nurturing a loved one is an effective way to speed recovery.

- Consider relationship counseling. Many rape crisis centers provide such services at little or no cost. A competent, sensitive counselor can help remove barriers to effective communication.

WHAT TO SAY TO OTHERS

Close family members often have responses which parallel those of the victim: shock, rage, confusion, guilt, and feelings of helplessness. It is important for them to express their feelings and to demonstrate their concern and support. However, well-intentioned efforts which create additional emotional burdens for her must be prevented. You may find yourself in the position of being a "buffer" between the woman and other family members. The following hints will help.

- Family members may seek to help the victim and alleviate their own feelings of helplessness by threatening revenge on the rapist. Again, such threats tend to further traumatize her and cause her to worry about the family's safety. Family members' anger can be expressed to you or a counselor, but should not be expressed to her. Constant expression of anger only heightens her anxiety and makes her feel guilty for "imposing" an emotional burden on those she loves.

- Discourage family and friends from unintentionally trivializing the sexual assault by joking about it. Male friends in particular may be prone to do this. Such jokes are likely to confuse and isolate her rather than being a means of raising her spirits.

- Well-intentioned family members may try to solicit support from close friends, clergy, co-workers and others. Such efforts should be discouraged if she is not prepared to discuss the incident. However, you should not prevent her from talking to family members if she chooses. She should decide to whom and under what circumstances to discuss her feelings.

- Family members should be dissuaded from overprotecting her. Strong attempts may be made to convince her to move back home, move to another city, or accept what amounts to twenty-four hour surveillance. The danger is that these actions may reinforce the woman's view of herself as vulnerable and powerless, thus discouraging her from mobilizing her own resources for coping. This can promote an unhealthy dependency on others. Providing support should not function to increase feelings that she has lost control over her life or that she is no longer self-reliant. If anything, family members need to understand that being supportive means helping her to build self-confidence and independence.

- Continual distraction of the victim should be discouraged. The family may engage in a "friendly conspiracy" to keep her mind off the incident, occupying her time with a variety of activities and acting as if it never happened. However, attempts to deny the rape are only temporarily effective and communicate that it is too awful to discuss or even to think about.

- Encourage family members to respect her need for privacy. There are times when it is desirable and therapeutic for her to work through feelings alone. A constant stream of well-wishers can drain her emotionally. It is especially difficult for her to put the incident behind her if she feels obliged to satisfy the frequent inquiries of visitors as to "what happened" and "how are you doing?" When she decides she needs to be alone, respect that decision. In addition, she may want you to communicate such decisions to the family for her. In doing so, you will assure family and friends that their concern is recognized and appreciated.

- No one should communicate that she was raped because she did something wrong. This is especially true in the case of teenagers who are victimized in the context of dating. Avoid suggesting that her actions, rather than the behavior of the rapist, are at fault. Furthermore, suggesting that she should have done things differently communicates more than blame or judgment of her. It also communicates that others do not fully understand the circumstances under which she was *forced* to act — circumstances which she didn't choose but which were imposed upon her.

Clearly, one of the chief tasks you face is to work with the victim's loved ones to provide a safe, accepting climate for her to release painful feelings without fear of criticism. And by letting her know that you trust her ability to recover, you help empower her to overcome what has happened.

4
Responding to Long-Term Consequences

We have described the woman's experience of rape and its immediate impact upon her. By now it should be apparent that the effects extend far beyond the episode and its immediate aftermath. A complete resolution of the incident may take months or even years to achieve. As time passes, there are a number of physical and psychological responses for which you should be prepared.

It was mentioned earlier that there is no such thing as a typical rape or rape victim. Likewise there is no such thing as a typical pattern of responses to rape. Some victims express their feelings openly, others attempt to control and hide them. Despite these individual differences, however, many counselors report that response to rape often follows a sequence referred to as the "Rape Trauma Syndrome." This "syndrome" is not a type of mental disorder, but a series of stages many (but not all) rape victims experience.

The first phase, acute distress, begins with the woman's responses immediately following the incident. These include shock, disbelief, confusion, anxiety, crying, and other signs of emotional disorganization. She may even appear to be extremely controlled on the surface, masking more troubling emotions at a deeper level. At the same time, a number of physical symptoms may appear: soreness and bruising from the attack, vaginal or rectal bleeding, tension headaches, fatigue, sleep disturbances (e.g., nightmares, insomnia, crying out in her sleep), stomach pains, nausea, lack of appetite, and vaginal infection.

The victim also experiences a variety of feelings in the weeks following the rape: fear, anger, embarrassment, and self-blame. Abrupt changes in mood are quite common. To compound her distress, she may feel she is overreacting to normal everyday problems and get angry with herself.

During this first phase, it is particularly important for you to remember that these physical and emotional reactions are *natural* responses to a terrifying, life-threatening experience. Let her know that these reactions are understandable and do not mean she is "going crazy."

The second phase is a period of apparent readjustment. That is, she may attempt to resolve her anxiety by rationalizing the rape. For example, she may announce that she has "forgotten" the incident, giving every outward appearance that it no longer troubles her. This may appear to be a final resolution, but typically is not. If anything, the rape is constantly in the background of her thoughts and has not been resolved. Keep in mind that this second phase *does* represent another step towards a true resolution of the incident.

The third phase, called reorganization or integration, is marked by the reemergence of a number of troubling responses experienced earlier (e.g., depression, anxiety, fear, insomnia, nightmares, tension headaches, etc.). Her emotional turmoil may surface in ways that are disquieting and perhaps unpredictable. Some victims become so depressed that they have suicidal thoughts. Many relationships undergo the greatest period of stress at this time because she appears to be "getting worse instead of better." These responses, while understandably disturbing, can be interpreted as a sign that she is beginning to confront and grapple with deep-seated feelings about the rape, feelings which she previously denied or rationalized.

Unfortunately, many victims incorrectly blame themselves for the rape. Feelings of guilt are common even though she is not to blame. Many rapists spend considerable time stalking their victims, waiting for an opportune moment when she is least able to resist. In order to help her deal with feelings of self-blame, it is important to convey to her four simple truisms about rape:

1. Regardless of where a woman is, no one has the right to rape her.

2. The fact that she may have been alone, dressed in a particular way, or may have been friendly to a person does not mean she deserved to be raped.

3. She is never responsible for the behavior of a rapist.

4. Most important, the fact that she survived the rape means that she did the right thing.

COPING WITH GRIEF

Grief is a natural response to personal loss which poses both challenges and opportunities. The challenges are especially complex if the grieving is due to being victimized by sexual assault. The initial shock following a rape often is replaced with an ill-defined but lingering feeling of grief among victims. This feeling of grief is due to the loss of one's sense of safety, trust, independence, and personal control.

The issue of grief recovery is particularly critical for husbands, fathers and male friends in their efforts to deal with loved ones in the aftermath of a rape. Rape victims are especially susceptible to the advice given to them by males whom they have come to trust. Unfortunately, much of the well-intentioned advice regarding how victims should and should not cope with rape reflects myth and folk wisdom rather than a sound understanding of the recovery process. Bad advice on how to cope is particularly worrisome because it can result in increased risk to the aggrieved. By understanding the myths and facts of grief recovery, males can be in a better position to offer practical suggestions to help loved ones.

Perhaps the most common misunderstanding regarding grief is that "time heals all wounds," and that time alone constitutes a magical potion which will somehow cover up deep feelings of loss. The problem is that simply "giving it time" does not necessarily resolve conflicts produced by the rape. To make matters worse, by telling a rape victim that only time will heal feelings of grief, you are unintentionally reinforcing feelings of powerlessness. Simply stated, it conveys the message that nothing you or anyone else does will relieve the emotional pain of rape, that one is ultimately alone in the suffering, and that inaction '(i.e., waiting) rather than action is the only way to cope.

Another misconception is that she "shouldn't think about it" or "shouldn't feel that way." Implied here are several unfortunate messages. First, by telling the victim not to dwell on the rape, you are telling her to ignore or to bury powerful feelings. Suppressing or ignoring feelings does not produce a sense of resolution, nor does it result in an emotional state which will allow the woman to get on with her life. Second, by telling an assault survivor not to feel a certain way, you are denying her the right to her feelings. You are also implying that she is somehow inadequate for not rationally controlling her emotional state, even though that is not the message you intend to communicate.

Such messages produce three unfortunate consequences. First, the woman in a state of grief begins to experience guilt for feeling (or not feeling) a certain way. This only adds to feelings of guilt which she already may be feeling. Second, the victim becomes very guarded in expressing to others how she truly feels out of fear of being judged, censored, or otherwise rejected. At a time when honest communication with loved ones is most critical, the woman feels unable to talk about what she is going through. Finally, encouraging victims of rape to bury their emotions only serves to confuse them as to their true feelings. Recovery from rape is accomplished when she feels free to be honest with herself and truly in touch with her feelings. Denial, guilt, and an inability to share feelings with others is a recipe for prolonging the anguish and limiting growth potential.

There are two common bits of folk wisdom which encourage rape victims to deny or suppress their feelings.

The first is to tell them to "keep busy." Immersion into work
or other activities does not magically cause one in a state of
grief to "snap out of it." Temporary distractions are just
that... temporary; they often serve to avoid or prolong
coming to terms with problems. Engaging in work, hobbies
or other activities while grieving has value to a point, so long
as it does not result in being isolated from sources of support
or in foregoing efforts to address the nature of one's feelings.
(The same is true when a person attempts to suppress grief
by medicating himself or herself into oblivion.)

The second piece of folk wisdom suggests that one can
diminish feelings of loss by acquiring something new. An
example of this is telling a child whose pet has died "not to
worry, you will be OK, we'll get you a new one." The obvious
problem is that grief caused by rape is not offset by new
possessions. Although well-intentioned, suggesting that
something new will somehow result in recovery may be
interpreted by her as trivializing her feelings. It may also be
interpreted as a crass attempt to buy off her sense of grief
and get her to act as if everything is back to normal. Little
wonder that many victims of rape learn to act as if they have
recovered, while continuing to suffer alone without fully
coming to terms with their victimization.

The problem of "acting recovered" is especially
common because the victim neither wants to burden others,
nor does she want to feel rejected because others do not
know how to respond to her. Both the victim and others may
"put on a happy face" to avoid confronting true feelings.
Because most people find it difficult to know how to respond
to another's grief, it becomes a simple thing for all
concerned to avoid the subject altogether. Complex feelings
of denial, guilt, anger, confusion and fear are then
compounded by this conspiracy of silence and the resulting
sense of isolation.

IMPACT ON MALES

Males often pass through a series of phases similar to those of the victim's Rape Trauma Syndrome. Included here are feelings of shock, confusion, intense anger, and feelings of guilt and self-blame for "failing to protect" a loved one. As a result, males also need to achieve resolution of the incident.

Many males whose loved ones have been raped feel a kind of "impotent rage" — wanting to strike out but having no appropriate means to do so. Your feelings of anger are a natural and common reaction. However, as we have already indicated, your feelings about the incident should be expressed to her in a gentle and calm manner, rather than in a state of extreme agitation or rage. This will keep the lines of communication open, a factor which is critical for the survival of your relationship with her.

Understanding and coping with anger is a key element in your mutual recovery. It is not uncommon for some of the intense anger men feel toward the rapist to be directed toward the victim. This transferring of anger is a gradual and subtle process, of which you may not even be aware. Directing anger toward the victim happens for a number of reasons, including the following:

- You may feel anger toward the victim because she has dependency needs which place additional demands on you. The turmoil caused by the incident taxes both of you emotionally, and it is likely that there are times when you may feel her need for understanding and patience is unrealistic or excessive. Ironically, oftentimes males initially encourage the victim to feel dependent on them,

then later come to resent what they believe is her
overdependence.

- You may feel that she is using her victimization as
a means of manipulating you and others. Perhaps
you feel that she is trying to draw attention to
herself, to elicit pity, or to use the incident to
avoid her responsibilities. If she does so, it is
probably not an attempt to manipulate and
control you; rather, it may be her way of regaining
the sense of personal control that was taken away
by her assailant.

- You may feel anger because her recovery is
progressing slower than you would like. You may
be frustrated because she doesn't seem to forget
the incident and to put it behind her. It is
important to remember that people recover at
different rates and in different ways. It is
unrealistic for you to impose on her the terms of
her recovery. Such an imposition communicates a
lack of understanding and is likely to be a source
of her feeling resentment toward you.

- As we mentioned earlier, some victims of sexual
assault are reluctant to talk about what happened.
Even though you feel that you are entitled to have
her confide in you, her reluctance to discuss the
incident should not incite you to anger. It does
not mean that she is "hiding" something or that
she does not trust you. Rather than being angry,
you could indicate to her that it is acceptable for
her to guard her feelings, and that you are ready
to listen patiently whenever she is ready to talk.

- After the initial shock, some males become angry toward the victim for "allowing" the incident to occur. This is especially true in the case of fathers whose adolescent daughters have been assaulted in a dating situation. Even if she had been drinking or had used poor judgment, blaming her for being irresponsible will only cause her to be angry with you. Ultimately, conveying feelings of anger and blame will close off communication and hinder your relationship.

COPING WITH ANGER

Unfortunately, there is no easy way for either of you to deal with these complex feelings. However, there are a number of guidelines which will help both of you.

- Do joint activities together which in the past have brought you closer together. Whether it be going for walks in nature, camping, gardening, or seeing films, the positive feelings associated with these activities helps to channel anger.

- Where appropriate and mutually agreed upon, seek the companionship of friends who are themselves healthy and up-beat. Being around positive people helps both of you to gain perspective.

- Do not act out in violent ways (e.g., destroying property, fighting, etc.) in the mistaken belief that violence is a cathartic or release for anger. Similarly, turning to alcohol or becoming a workaholic does not eliminate feelings of anger and only serves to isolate the victim.

- Agreeing to pretend that the rape never happened does not end the anger. If anything, such a pretense promotes emotional dishonesty and poor communication. It is acceptable to be honest with yourself and with your loved one that anger about the incident is one of the feelings you are experiencing. Being emotionally honest is a sign of trust in the other and encourages honesty in return.

- Victims, and especially their male loved ones, are likely to experience "revenge fantasies." Such fantasies are normal and should be acknowledged. However, dwelling on them and letting these fantasies dominate your communications is counterproductive.

- Perhaps the most important way for the two of you to gain control of the complex feelings you are experiencing is to find a trusted person with whom you can talk. Seeking a good friend, or counselor, or minister allows you to talk about what you are feeling without fear of being judged. For some, it is especially useful to locate survivors groups where members meet regularly to discuss their experiences associated with sexual assault. Knowing that others have endured what the two of you are going through helps you to release pent-up emotional energy.

Remember that each person has developed his or her own ways of coping with emotional stress. Share your feelings with each other but don't expect her methods of coping to be identical to yours.* With mutual support and openness, you both will recover and you may succeed in building a relationship with her which is even stronger than before.

---

*We strongly recommend that she read a companion volume to this book written for rape victims. The book is entitled *If You Are Raped* by Kathryn M. Johnson, Learning Publications, Inc.

5
Overcoming Fears About Sex

One of the consequences of rape is considerable anxiety concerning sexual activity. For a young victim this may be her first sexual experience, causing her great confusion about human sexuality. For all victims, rape is done in a violent context devoid of love and emotional intimacy. Such an experience may result in a long-term fear of sexual involvement, or increase sexual difficulties that already existed between partners.

For men who are the sexual partners of rape victims, there is likely to be a temporary disruption of sexual activity. Difficulties may be especially acute if the rape was extremely violent or involved multiple rapists. Most victims experience changes in their sexual responsiveness, and are concerned about the responses of their partners.

It is not uncommon for a rape victim to experience flashbacks during sexual relations. If you are insensitive to her needs, it may make the resumption of sex seem rape-like, reminding her of the incident. Likewise, males are often insecure about their sexual performance, especially if she

seems reluctant or unresponsive. In other words, both
partners normally experience complex feelings about sexual
impulses following a rape. As her partner, you should ask
yourself, "How can I effectively communicate with the
woman I love when she has been sexually assaulted?" The
following suggestions will help.

- She needs to be given every opportunity to regain
  her sense of personal control, especially in the
  area of sexual decision making. Do not demand
  or pressure her into sexual activity. Resuming sex
  is not necessarily a means of normalizing the
  relationship or of helping her to recover. Let her
  make sexual decisions, especially if she needs a
  period of abstinence.

- Don't be angry with her or doubt your adequacy if
  she appears less responsive than before. It may be
  that certain cues present during the rape (e.g., the
  smell of alcohol) inhibit her responsiveness. A
  willingness to alter patterns will help your
  relationship.

- Just as you should not pressure her into an early
  resumption of sex, neither should you avoid any
  display of intimacy. Understandably, some males
  assume that victims will have a diminished interest
  in sex and they therefore emotionally withdraw
  from her. It is important that she doesn't
  misinterpret your behavior as a sign that you feel
  she is "tarnished." There are many ways to
  express intimacy without consummating that
  intimacy sexually. For example, asking permission
  to hold or cuddle her is appropriate. Again,

honest communication and a willingness to take your cues from her will help your relationship.

- Some males experience erotic feelings when the victim describes the rape to them, and then feel guilty for having such feelings. This merely demonstrates the fact that rape produces a variety of conflicting emotions in people. If you do feel aroused when learning of the incident, *do not* communicate these feelings to the victim because this will only provoke greater anxiety in her. If such feelings persist, it would be valuable to seek the assistance of a counselor.

- Be patient. Sexual disruption following rape is usually temporary and can be overcome with sensitivity and understanding.

A SPECIAL WORD TO FATHERS

When the victim of sexual assault is a child or adolescent, the emotional impact on her and her family is especially severe. Fathers, who have a strong sense of responsibility for the safety of their daughters, may have particularly intense reactions such as rage and self-blame. In the crucial hours and days following the rape, however, it is absolutely critical that you be aware of the stresses on your child. The following should be kept in mind:

- Rape may have been your daughter's first sexual experience, causing her to have exaggerated fears about adult intimacy. She needs to know that she is not tarnished, that her capacity for adult intimacy is not diminished, and that rape is not how loving couples express themselves sexually.

She also needs to understand that rape is a crime
of violence, not an act of "uncontrolled passion,"
and that she bears no responsibility for the
violence inflicted upon her.

- Because many fathers find it difficult to discuss
  sexuality with their daughters, a sympathetic and
  knowledgeable person (e.g., nurse or counselor)
  should be available to answer her questions. A
  refusal to divulge information about human
  sexuality when that information is sought by the
  victim will only heighten her fears. Honest
  responses to her questions help her to gain control
  and to reduce her confusion.

- If the victim is an adolescent, the rape may
  compound communication problems which already
  exist. Do not force her to self-disclose, but if she
  expresses a desire to talk about the assault, be
  prepared to do so. She can benefit from talking
  about the experience, if it is *her* decision to talk.
  Attempts to help your child "forget" about the
  rape by refusing to discuss it may give her the
  impression that you are ashamed of her or hold
  her responsible.

- If she was raped by a date, she is likely to fear that
  you will hold her responsible for using poor
  judgment. She may fear that she will be punished,
  that she will not be believed, or that you will take
  matters into your own hands and cause her to be
  ostracized by her peers. In anticipation of your
  responses, she may conceal information from you,
  or otherwise act out in ways which further
  undermine her credibility. Again, it is important

for you not to judge or punish her for what happened. Equally important, do not display more concern for what others might think (i.e., family reputation) than for your daughter's recovery needs. Knowing that she does not have to fear your reactions will be a positive step in her recovery.

- Encourage your daughter to resume her normal lifestyle. Limiting your daughter's emerging independence by making decisions for her, or "grounding" her for not being sufficiently careful, may seem like punishment and should be avoided. It is also important that her rights concerning dating, seeing friends, involvement in extracurricular events at school, as well as her responsibilities for household chores, remain the same. If she is overprotected or allowed to avoid routine activities, she will have a more lengthy and difficult period of readjustment.

- If the victim is a young child, she may express herself behaviorally, rather than verbally. Be alert for changes such as loss of appetite, withdrawal, altered sleeping patterns, nightmares, or fear of being alone. These reactions are quite common but should be monitored closely for frequency and severity.

- If the crime is reported to the authorities and the victim is a child, parental permission may be required for medical treatment and police questioning. Be available to provide such authorizations and any additional information needed by medical and police personnel.

- The gynecological exam may also be a first-time experience and can be extremely upsetting unless parents and medical staff are sensitive. Gently convince her that the procedure is necessary, but insist that the medical staff carry out the exam with patience and sensitivity.

We have already pointed out that blaming the victim or making threats of revenge against the rapist are counterproductive and should be avoided. We want to emphasize again that you should not hold yourself responsible for the rape or for failing to protect her. It is virtually impossible to create an environment in which the possibility of rape is completely eliminated. Instead of worrying about who is to blame for the incident, concentrate your energy on helping your daughter to complete physical and emotional recovery.

6
Understanding
Acquaintance Rape

The number of acquaintance rapes committed each year is staggering. Although statistics vary, it has been estimated that 70% to 80% of all rape victims are attacked by someone they know. The nature of the victim-offender relationship exists on a continuum from slight acquaintance to former husband or lover. In a great many cases, rape occurs in the context of a dating relationship or, if a child is the victim, within the family. While adult victims over age twenty-five have a somewhat greater likelihood of being raped by a total stranger, children, adolescents and college-age females are most likely to be victimized by a person who is known.

Just as rape by a total stranger is traumatic and frightening, so too is assault by someone who is known and trusted. Consider the situation of many teenagers and college students whose active social lives regularly involve them in school activities, parties and other settings where they are in contact with a variety of males. There is a tendency among females to assume that such settings are a safe way of meeting new friends and potential dating partners. In such encounters, where she comes to know someone at least casually, it is normal and understandable to presume a certain degree of trust and to want to be on good terms. As a consequence of her good intentions and a desire to be sociable, her trust is used against her and she is placed at great risk.

Many males, despite their best efforts, have a difficult time comprehending how a woman can be raped by someone she knows. To facilitate the understanding of acquaintance rape, some researchers and counselors (e.g., Py Bateman, director of Alternatives to Fear in Seattle, Washington) find it useful to characterize the crime as a three stage process.

1. **INTRUSION:** Often the offender begins by somehow violating his victim's space. Examples of intrusions include interrupting her when she is speaking, unwanted touches, or conversations about things she would rather not talk about because they are too personal. Usually the intrusions first take place in a way that is not directly threatening, but nevertheless make her feel uncomfortable.

2. **DESENSITIZATION:** In this stage, the victim gets used to the intrusions. She starts to think "that's just the way he is," that he doesn't mean anything by it, and that there is really nothing wrong with the way he acts. She isn't sensitive to the intrusions anymore and may drop her guard.

3. **ISOLATION:** The offender attempts to get the victim alone. He also consciously uses strategies which somehow compromise her (e.g., by giving her alcohol).

Isolation can occur in a variety of settings, including some (e.g., her home) in which the victim might believe she is completely safe.

4. To these, we would add a fourth stage: **OFFENDER DENIAL.** Invariably, an offender will claim that the victim gave consent and invited his "attentions." His denials serve to justify his actions to himself and others, and also serve to reinforce his victim's feelings of guilt and confusion.

While these stages do not always occur, they serve as a reminder that even those who are cautious and attempt to exercise good judgment can be at risk.

The following sequence of events illustrates the dynamics involved in many cases. A young woman is introduced to a "friend of a friend" at a party. Since he appears to her to be "a decent guy," she accepts his invitation to go out with another couple for something to eat, even though the way he looks at her makes her feel vaguely uncomfortable (intrusion). Because she has no reason to suspect his motives, she invites him to her apartment for an after-dinner drink. Whether misinterpreting her friendliness or because of more sinister motives, the guy makes physical advances toward her. Assuming that this is, for him, typical behavior (desensitization), the woman politely puts up with his initial advances and gently tries to dissuade him. Her desire to spare his feelings and the belief that she can control the situation actually work to her disadvantage as she delays taking any protective action. Now that he has her alone, (isolation), his behavior becomes progressively more aggressive. Finally, she becomes insistent and demands that he stop. It is at this point that the man becomes verbally abusive (e.g., calling her a "bitch") and uses physical force to impose his will upon her. Afterward, he asks her why she invited him to her apartment if she didn't wish to have sexual intercourse with him (offender denial).

Unfortunately, episodes of this nature occur at an alarming rate in the context of dating relationships. Given such an experience, not only has the woman become the victim of a sexual assault, but she is often left with a lingering feeling that she is somehow responsible for using poor judgment or for failing to control his "natural urges." Little wonder that victims of acquaintance rape characteristically experience confusion and guilt. It is also not surprising that victims of this form of sexual assault are *least* likely to report it to the police.

In part, the victim's confusion stems from widely held beliefs in our culture that after a certain degree of intimacy (e.g., kissing or petting), males have sexual rights over a woman regardless of her objections. Thus the burden is placed on the female to recognize at what point he can no longer control *his* "urges," implying that she is responsible for his aggressiveness and lack of self-control.

The psychological effects of acquaintance rape on the victim may be somewhat different that the effects of rape by a complete stranger. We do not mean to imply that the consequences are less serious. If anything, some of the emotional consequences are likely to be felt *more* intensely in cases where the victim and offender are known to one another. Because she has been violated by someone she trusted, she may now believe that she is a poor judge of character. It is common for her to experience self-doubt and apprehension, especially when meeting new people. This lack of faith in her own judgment may gradually develop into a generalized distrust of *all* males, including close friends who are worthy of trust.

In addition, the victim may feel that by not refusing his advances sooner or more firmly, she somehow bears partial responsibility for "triggering" in him these "uncontrollable" desires. Such deeply felt confusion over her judgment and responsibility is intensified by mutual friends who claim that "he's not that kind of guy." In many cases the victim is cut off from the support of family and friends because she remains silent out of fear that others will not believe she was assaulted, or worse, will claim that she provoked him. To the extent that the rapist has friends within the same social network as the victim, her potential support system is likely to be undermined and her version of events called into question. It is this lack of support that has negative consequences for her emotional adjustment and decreases the likelihood of her pursuing legal action.

If the victim decides to take legal action against an assailant who is known to her, the emotional difficulties she experiences may be compounded. Police frequently express reluctance to pursue criminal cases where evidence is perceived to be difficult to obtain, or if they believe that charges will be dropped when the case goes to trial. Because conclusive evidence is often difficult to produce in rape investigations, the police may view the victim's claim as unsubstantiated or impossible to prove in court. Acquaintance rape, particularly if it involves a former lover or ex-husband, is likely to be dismissed by police as an "unfounded" charge and therefore not worth the time and trouble to investigate. The reasons for unfounding charges of rape against acquaintances include:

1. a tendency to view the reported episode as a "lover's quarrel" rather than as a serious sexual assault;

2. a belief that she will drop all charges after she has had time to "cool down";

3. if kissing or sexual foreplay occurred prior to the assault, a belief that she "assumed the risk" and gave tacit consent to intercourse;

4. a belief that the victim is promiscuous, a "pick-up," or that she intentionally was being seductive or a "tease";

5. because of prior sexual involvement with the man (e.g., an ex-husband), a belief that she is exaggerating or lying in order to seek revenge;

6. lack of physical evidence (e.g., bruises, abrasions), medical reports, or eyewitness accounts wherein the charge of rape becomes her word against his;

7. witnesses who know both parties and whose testimony might cast doubt on her version of events.

In a very real sense, police response (or rather lack of response) to her claim that she was raped by an acquaintance further contributes to her victimization. Although more will be said about this in a separate chapter, actions taken by the police and courts can unintentionally add to her frustration and anxiety. The tendency of others not to believe she was raped, or that she is being untruthful, functions to increase her sense of guilt, confusion and anger.

There are several ways you can demonstrate your support and affection if she has been sexually assaulted by an acquaintance and decides to press charges against him.

- It is of vital importance to reassure her that you believe her story, regardless of the actions of police or others who are aware of the incident.

- To counter the self-doubts about her ability to judge character, you must convince her of a simple fact—it is impossible to know in advance who will be a rapist. Neighbors, friends, fellow employees, former partners and new acquaintances are all potential assailants and may need only the right opportunity for rape to occur.

- Remind her that even if she was initially friendly to the rapist, she absolutely is not responsible for causing him to "lose control." Demonstrations of affection and friendship on her part do not make her liable for his aggressive actions.

- It is important for you to diffuse the generalized feeling of distrust she may have developed. Such apprehension can function to isolate her and greatly hamper her future interactions with others. She needs to feel that her assailant is not representative of all males and that trust is an essential prerequisite for developing healthy, intimate relationships. Indeed, your relationship with her should illustrate the value of openness and trust.

- Finally, regardless of whether she presses charges, encourage her to get medical attention and to call a rape crisis center. These steps will help initiate the recovery process.

Acquaintance rape also is likely to produce particularly strong emotional reactions in you. If the rapist is an acquaintance or friend of yours, you probably will feel a violation of trust or question your own judgment of character. Moreover, husbands and male partners of the victim often have friends who operate in the same social circle as the rapist. This can be very awkward for you, the woman, and those mutual friends and acquaintances who wish to avoid taking sides. Furthermore, rumors about the rapist's version of events, as well as general gossip about the reputation of both rapist and victim, may become frequent topics of conversation and continually confront you and her. This is especially true if the victim and assailant are still attending school.

As we have indicated elsewhere, it is totally inappropriate and even dangerous for you to seek revenge against the rapist, even if he is known to you and could be located without difficulty. In addition, if mutual acquaintances remain on good terms with the assailant, it may create doubts in your mind. It is a sure bet that the rapist will deny everything. In fact, in acquaintance rape cases, the most frequently used defenses are that the victim consented to have sex, or that no sexual activity occurred. You might begin to think, "After all, if the people we know still think he is OK, maybe it didn't happen the way she said." Given such thinking, it is possible you will feel that she is partially to blame, or that he is a sexual rival.

While such thoughts are understandable, they represent a distorted view of what has taken place. Regardless of any gossip you may hear, your assessment of events should reflect the realization that she is the victim, not the perpetrator. Your love relationship with her, not casual contacts with others, should be the basis for understanding what has transpired. In short, don't let others inadvertently

jeopardize the trust and understanding that is the basis of
your relationship with her. In light of these complexities
surrounding acquaintance rape, it would be helpful for you
to keep in mind the points which follow.

- No woman wants to be forced into sexual
  relations, and the rapist, even if he is an
  acquaintance, is not your rival.

- You cannot control what others think or say about
  the incident. Your belief in her and your support
  for her are what matter.

- Do not feel guilty if an element of doubt crosses
  your mind. Such thoughts are not unusual but
  almost certainly are based on false assumptions.

- Neither you nor the victim are in any way
  responsible for what happens to the assailant if
  charges are filed with the police. It is the
  responsibility of the courts to decide his fate,
  regardless of any pressure that parents or friends
  of the rapist may bring to bear upon the victim or
  you.

- Do not isolate yourself or her from friends who
  know of the rape. Neither she nor you have any
  reason to feel shame, embarrassment, or guilt.
  Remember that your true friends will be
  understanding and supportive.

In summary, the consequences of acquaintance rape
pose difficulties for the victim as well as for you. However,
you can hasten her recovery by letting her know that you

believe her, by communicating openly and honestly with her, and by demonstrating your love and support for her.

7
Special Cases: Dealing with Interracial and Gang Rape

$\mathbf{A}$lthough the majority of rapes are between persons of the same race, it has been estimated that approximately ten to twenty percent of reported rapes are interracial (e.g., black male-white female, white male-black female). The crime statistics suggest that reported interracial rapes more often involve black assailants and white victims. However, the key word is "reported." There is evidence that black women, perhaps out of a belief that the police will not conduct a vigorous investigation of the complaint, are unlikely to report rapes if the assailant is white.

In any event, interracial rape tends to evoke especially strong feelings of outrage from those close to the victim. If expressed in her presence, these feelings may further confuse and traumatize her. In addition, the victim's own responses to interracial rape often are organized around racial themes. If so, her psychological recovery may be impeded. It is therefore important that you understand the dynamics of interracial rape. Be prepared to deal with reactions of the victim and those close to her which might hinder a healthy resolution of the incident.

It should be noted that the complications involved in this form of sexual assault are not strictly limited to race. Indeed, the same recovery problems can be associated with various ethnic or religious groups, or even persons of different social classes.

In cases of interracial rape, the assailant is typically a stranger. Perhaps this is because casual social contact (e.g., having a drink in a bar), which often precedes rape, may be frowned upon and is thus less likely to occur when males and females are of different races. Since social norms tend to restrict the access of rapists to victims of different races, interracial rapes occur in settings where the victim is accessible and vulnerable. The victim may be seized in a park, on a street corner as she waits for a bus, while out shopping, or as she returns home from school or work. Very often a weapon is used to force her to submit. Many of these attacks occur in broad daylight as the woman performs the tasks which make up her daily routine. Consider the following scenario.

Jane, a black female, is in the midst of her daily three mile jog through the city. As she enters a residential area which adjoins her own neighborhood, she is suddenly knocked to the ground by a white assailant. A knife is placed to her throat and she is forced into a nearby alley and raped. Afterward, she is released and manages to get to her home, where she tells her husband of the assault. What kinds of reactions might Jane have to the rape? The following are quite common:

- She might conclude that the rape was racially motivated. This is particularly likely in areas where considerable interracial tensions already exist or if verbal abuse from the rapist contained references to the victim's race.

- Since Jane is black and her assailant was white, she may have to spend additional time weighing the pros and cons of reporting the rape to the authorities. Often members of a racial minority lack confidence in a legal system which they feel may not represent their interests.

- Her anger towards the rapist may now generalize to all members of his race. As a result, rather than coming to grips with her feelings about this specific person, she "resolves" the incident by concluding that **all** white males (or black males, if the victim is white and the assailant is black) are rapists.

- Related to the above, the victim may develop distrust and fear of all members of that race, experiencing anxiety and panic whenever they are in the general vicinity. Because daily activities often involve interracial contact, such reactions can be a serious impediment to her recovery.

- Relationships with friends and acquaintances who are of the same race as the assailant may be affected adversely. Some women find themselves avoiding such acquaintances and therefore lose a portion of their social support system at a time when they most need it.

These kinds of reactions, especially ones which involve generalized anger towards all members of the assailant's race, are also experienced by males close to the victim. Keep in mind that focusing on the assailant's race distracts the victim from the real issue — her feelings about *that particular person*. To help her respond in a way which promotes a healthy resolution of the incident, there are several important points to keep in mind.

- Family and friends must be dissuaded from making racial slurs. Such comments may encourage her to attribute causality for the rape to the assailant's race, and thus keep her from coming to grips with her feelings toward the *individual* who assaulted her.

- Remind her that not all male members of that race are rapists. If she has close friends or acquaintances of that race, point out to her that these individuals have been and will continue to be deserving of her trust and friendship. If you notice her avoiding contact with these acquaintances, you can suggest that she discuss this with her counselor, if she is seeing one.

- Reassure her that she did *not* put herself in a situation where rape could occur, that you do not hold her responsible for the assault, and that you in no way consider her to be "unclean" because she was raped by a member of another race.

- Since interracial rape so frequently occurs while the victim is in the midst of her daily activities, you must encourage her to resume those activities as soon as possible. Her attempts to prevent another assault by staying home from school, avoiding shopping trips, or simply refusing to venture out of the home will prevent her from reestablishing a sense of freedom.

Remember that even if the rape *appears* to be racially motivated, race is not the central issue in her victimization. The violence, injury, and degradation that one human imposes upon another is the real tragedy of rape and should be the focus of your efforts to help her.

GANG RAPE

Until recently, little was known about gang rape (that is, an assault involving multiple offenders). However, intense media coverage of gang rapes in New Bedford, Massachusetts and New York City's Central Park has heightened public concern about gang rape and its effects on victims. What has been learned is that gang rapes are likely to be even more violent and traumatizing than single offender assaults. Compared to single offender rapes, gang rapes are more likely to involve physical violence, the use of a weapon, and acts which meet the legal definition of rape. Also, gang rape victims tend to see their offenders as more aggressive, feel more scared during the attack, and are more likely than single offender victims to contemplate suicide following the incident.

Gang rape is therefore a particularly frightening and degrading experience, but there are steps you can take to lessen the impact of the assault on the victim. For example, because gang rapes tend to be even more violent and traumatizing than single offender rapes, it is essential that she receive immediate medical attention. In addition, psychological help – which can be obtained by contacting the local rape crisis center – will probably be needed to help her deal with the immediate aftermath, and you can help by encouraging her to seek such assistance.

If the offenders are acquaintances of the victim, other kinds of complications may result. For example, the assailants will undoubtedly claim—as a group—that the victim consented to have sex with them. For example, there are cases where fraternity members, members of a team, or even gang members claim that the victim agreed to have intercourse with the group. In other words, they collectively shift responsibility away from themselves to the victim. It therefore becomes their word against hers.

Furthermore, because many acquaintance gang rapes occur during or after parties (hence the term "party" rape), the police may see the incident as "group sex," rather than rape. Gang rape victims who are high school or college students are particularly likely to be blamed for their victimization, and must suffer the additional trauma of encountering their assailants daily on the campus or school grounds. The incident is also likely to become common knowledge via the campus grapevine.

For these reasons, it is particularly important for you to let her know that you believe her, that you will support whatever actions she may choose to take against the assailants, and that you will help her withstand attempts by the offenders and their friends to intimidate her into dropping charges. It is also important that you do not initiate legal action against an organization (e.g., a fraternity or a school) if it is contrary to the victim's wishes. Such lawsuits have a high probability of publicizing the event and of causing people to choose sides in the matter. The victim should be made aware of both the costs and the possible benefits of a civil suit, and no action should be taken unless she gives her consent.

8
Reporting the Rape

Although it is a serious crime, rape frequently goes unreported. The FBI estimates that perhaps no more than one in ten rapes is ever reported to the police. The reasons given by victims for not reporting rapes to the police include:

- having had a prior relationship with the assailant;

- in cases of acquaintance rape, confusion as to whether a rape occurred and, if so, a feeling of responsibility that she somehow caused the rape or "allowed" it to happen;

- a feeling that nothing can be done or it can't be proven that rape occurred;

- a feeling that rape is too personal for others to know about;

- an unwillingness to be subjected to the legal system; and

- a fear of reprisal.

In addition, for reasons discussed in this chapter, many reported rapes never go to trial. However, out of a desire that the rapist be punished or out of fear that he will attack others, an increasing number of women are willing to testify against their assailants. We believe that such a decision is especially courageous, given that a rape trial is both anxiety-producing and psychologically exhausting for many victims.

We believe also that the decision whether or not to press charges should be made *by the victim*, and that you should fully support her decision, whatever it may be. In order to provide maximum support for her, it is important that you understand the various procedures initiated when the assault is reported (summarized in a chart on the final page of this chapter) and the implications of her decision to pursue legal action.

The collection of evidence for a rape trial begins with a preliminary police interview and a medical examination directly following the rape episode. The sooner the police are notified, the greater the likelihood of obtaining solid evidence. However, reporting to the police merely gives the victim the option of later prosecution if she decides to pursue the case. After she gives an initial report to uniformed officers, perhaps at the emergency room, the victim must undergo a medical examination to confirm that a sexual assault has taken place. This exam, which is conducted *before* she is allowed to bathe and change clothing, may entail a lengthy wait in a hospital emergency room followed by a pelvic exam, test for venereal disease, vaginal, oral, and rectal swabs, pubic combing, fingernail scrapings, and treatment for any injuries she may have suffered.

As you can well imagine, this kind of exam, carried out by strangers in the immediate aftermath of a life-threatening episode, is extremely unsettling. One way you can help is by requesting that the exam be performed by a "rape team," if the facility has one. These teams usually consist of medical professionals and counselors trained to collect the evidence efficiently and in a manner which is responsive to the emotional needs of the victim. Also, ask for a private waiting area for her, so that she doesn't have to sit in the emergency room waiting area. Finally, you can help by being available to answer questions that might arise.

Shortly thereafter, a detective will be assigned to the case and arrangements will be made for the victim to give a statement. In addition to giving and signing the statement, the victim may be asked to identify weapons or other evidence collected by the police, help construct a composite sketch of the assailant, and examine books of "mug" shots.

Rape victims do not always call the police immediately after the incident. Because you are loved and trusted by her, you may be the first person to whom she speaks about being raped. If this is the case, your immediate concern is to make certain she receives medical attention as soon as possible. There are two important reasons for an immediate medical examination. First, she may have suffered serious injuries other than obvious external cuts and bruises (e.g., internal bleeding). Second, police see medical evidence as crucial in establishing that a rape occurred (although in many acquaintance rape cases, the assailant freely admits that sexual intercourse occurred, but argues that it was consensual). The longer the delay between the assault and the examination, the more difficult it is to secure this evidence.

In addition to ensuring that she receives proper medical care, being the first person to hear of her victimization has another important implication. If she reports the rape to the police, you very likely will be asked to provide them with your own statement in addition to hers. She may have told you details that she failed to recall when later questioned by the police. Furthermore, if the case goes to trial, you stand a good chance of serving as a witness on behalf of the state. If indeed you endure lengthy questioning by police, the rape victim may feel an added responsibility for "dragging you into this situation." It is important for you to convey to her that your concern is for her well-being and that your assisting the police is only a minor inconvenience, especially if it means punishing the assailant.

Given the deeply personal and sensitive nature of rape evidence, being questioned by the police is usually emotionally draining for the victim. However, there are several ways to help reduce her emotional burden:

- She may request that you be present when she discusses the incident with investigators. Being with her at this moment can provide reassurance and make her feel less isolated. However, it is *very* important that you do not interrupt her account of events or interfere with police questioning. Despite your good intentions, it is not helpful for you to answer questions for her.

- She may request that you *not* be present during police questioning. Such reluctance to disclose to you details of the rape during police interviews does not mean she is disregarding your feelings. It should be her decision to discuss the rape with you on her terms, at a time she feels is appropriate, without strangers being present. Respect her wishes in this matter and do not feel that she is slighting you.

- Many women feel more comfortable if a female police officer is present or is conducting the questioning. If such a person is available, remind the victim to request her presence for the duration of the questioning.

- Most victims do not know what to expect when being questioned by police and are unclear as to why so many people are involved in obtaining information. Standard police procedures can create confusion for those not acquainted with their routines. Whenever possible, make sure that the police explain to the victim why they are proceeding in a particular fashion. Asking questions about what they do is not an implied criticism, but rather a way to reduce the understandable confusion she is experiencing.

- Because of the lengthy nature of most police interviews, she may have gone without food for a long period. If she is hungry, make sure that she is able to have a hot meal.

After questioning, the police will attempt to locate and arrest the suspect, if one has been identified. They will also contact the district attorney to discuss prosecution of the case. The police may advise against prosecution; that is, the rape complaint may be designated as "unfounded." The term unfounded can mean two things: 1) the police do not believe the charge is valid; or 2) they see it as valid but not likely to result in a successful prosecution. In the latter case, they believe her, but don't think they can get a conviction. Some reasons for "unfounding" a complaint are:

- delay in reporting by the victim;

- previous victim-assailant relationship (e.g., former lovers);

- evidence that the victim was intoxicated or using illicit drugs;

- refusal to undergo the medical examination;

- failure to preserve relevant physical evidence (e.g., douching before reporting the crime);

- "victim precipitation" (e.g., hitchhiking, walking alone at night in a rough neighborhood, withdrawing from a previous agreement to have sexual relations);

- victim alters her story after filing charges;

- circumstances associated with the incident are atypical or do not fit a "standard pattern" commonly found by investigators, thus raising the suspicion that she is lying;

- victim is hostile toward police or is perceived to be uncooperative.

In addition to the reasons listed above, a victim may be discouraged from filing charges if the police simply doubt her credibility as a witness; that is, if her appearance and "lifestyle" are such that the police and district attorney feel her case would be difficult to prove in court. The police often have a mental profile of whom they consider ideal or poor witnesses. Such factors as reputation, relationship to assailant (e.g., ex-lover vs. total stranger), and whether or not the victim abuses drugs or alcohol, influence how the police will respond to the complaint.

If the police and district attorney agree that a crime has been committed, but that it is not a "good" rape case, they may decide to prosecute the assailant on charges other than rape. In fact, rape is only one category under the broad heading of "sexual assaults." These categories can include: rape, attempted rape, sexual battery, corruption of a minor, gross sexual imposition, importuning, voyeurism, and public indecency. Furthermore, the authorities may decide to file charges on a number of other offenses which seem incidental to the assault (e.g., breaking and entering, burglary, aggravated robbery), if they feel there is strong evidence.

Filing charges sets in motion a lengthy and emotionally draining legal process wherein the truth and accuracy of the victim's story may repeatedly be called into question. Once the charges have been filed, the crime is viewed as an action against the state, with the woman serving as a witness on behalf of the state. The judicial system thus tends to depersonalize what is to the woman a singularly terrifying experience. Furthermore, what seems to the woman to be personal medical information now becomes part of the public record. (To the extent possible, you should work to preserve the woman's right to privacy by attempting to have her name withheld from newspaper accounts.) Shortly after charges are filed, depending upon the laws in that particular jurisdiction, the victim may be asked to testify before a grand jury, which determines if there is enough evidence to indict the accused. If the victim fails to appear in court for this preliminary hearing, charges against the assailant may be dropped.

Once the victim completes this process, she may be called upon in the future to provide additional information. At some point, she should ask to see the police follow-up reports on her case. This is a useful means of ensuring that they accurately represented her position and have a complete account of the incident. You may also request that the court protect the victim from unwanted contacts by the defense attorney or family and friends of the rapist. Finally, you should inquire whether there is a victim compensation or restitution program in your state or community. Such programs can help to compensate victims for medical or other expenses incurred as a result of being raped.

Keep in mind that this is an extremely trying time for the victim. She has by now recounted the incident to a number of *individuals*, but on this occasion she will be describing the details of the assault to a group of approximately 12 people (the grand jury, judge, district attorney, court reporter), almost all of whom are strangers. You can help her through this difficult time by reassuring her that her decision to pursue legal action is the proper one, by rehearsing her grand jury testimony with her, and by doing whatever you can to help her stay calm and composed as the time for her testimony approaches.

REPORTING A SEXUAL ASSAULT: TYPICAL PROCEDURES

The Immediate Aftermath

- Reporting of incident to police

- Initial police interview

- Medical examination

The Next Day

- Official statement given to police

- Identification of weapons or other evidence collected by police

- Identification of assailant (construction of composite sketch, examination of "mug shots")

- Polygraph exam (not mandatory)

- Charges filed

Apprehension of Suspect

- Testimony before grand jury

- Assailant indicted, trial date set (3 to 9 months after indictment)

9
Going to Trial

Once the assailant has been indicted, there is typically a three to nine month waiting period before the trial begins. This is a particularly difficult time for the woman for several reasons. First, her assailant may post bond and hence remain free to "walk the streets." She is likely to experience an understandable fear that he will seek revenge, although restraining orders should help protect her from this possibility. Also, family and friends of the rapist may call her and attempt to persuade her to drop the charges. Likewise, the defense attorney may attempt a number of delay tactics in the hope that she will not pursue the case. Perhaps most important of all, the woman is placed in a position of having to keep the incident in the forefront of her consciousness, remembering all of the details, until after the trial. In other words, during the pre-trial period she is given little opportunity to put the incident behind her and get on with her life.

THE PRE-TRIAL PERIOD

This pre-trial period requires great patience, understanding and support on your part. She may exhibit a number of physiological and emotional patterns which you find distressing (e.g., nightmares, insomnia, loss of appetite, fatigue, depression, tension headaches, and generalized anxiety). It is at this point that your relationship with her may undergo the greatest stress. It is not uncommon for some men to feel annoyed at her for being "too emotional" and insist that she cease talking and thinking about it. Some men develop a sense of resentment toward the woman for having to spend increased time with her or because she seems unresponsive to the man's needs. Patience on your part is important at this time; it can only add to the quality of your relationship in the long run. We urge you to keep in mind two things.

1. She did not choose this situation and feelings of anger and resentment will only add to her distress.

2. The difficult period she is going through is temporary and is likely to gradually diminish once the trial has ended.

A common experience among victims waiting for the rape trial to begin is a considerable degree of apprehension about serving as a witness. Such anxiety is normal and understandable when one considers the fact that many victims have never even seen the inside of a courtroom, much less having to speak into a microphone in front of a group of strangers. Her anxiety may be compounded if there is poor communication from the police and district attorney's office concerning the dynamics of the legal process and what is expected of her as a witness.

Furthermore, like most people, she may have only a vague idea of standard courtroom procedures, the meaning of legal and medical jargon relevant to the case, or proper courtroom decorum when testifying. Little wonder if she has serious doubts about wanting to endure a trial.

To make matters worse, victims frequently come to feel that they are pawns in a legal chess game where they have no power to decide things which affect them directly. There are seemingly endless delays in finally bringing the case to trial. Typically the defense attorney will *deliberately* seek court delays as a tactic to discourage the victim. This is especially difficult for witnesses who must rearrange work schedules or travel from a long distance to testify. You should do all you can to encourage the district attorney to demand a speedy trial. The victim should have a right to protection against frivolous requests for delays. Likewise, the district attorney should be discouraged from making decisions about her case without consulting her. Unfortunately, most of her contact with the police and district attorney's office will be at their convenience, not hers. In a very real sense, the impersonal character of the legal system can function to dehumanize the rape victim and further strain her emotional resources.

In order to help her regain a sense of control and prepare her for what to expect in court, there are a number of things you can do. Although no two cases are exactly alike, the following suggestions are of use in helping her prepare for trial.

- Encourage her to request from the district attorney a copy of her signed statement given to the police shortly after the incident. This statement is important evidence and reviewing it will refresh her memory of the event. If there are discrepancies between this statement and subsequent courtroom testimony, the defense attorney may claim she is an unreliable witness in an attempt to discredit her. It is very important that she remember the detailed sequence of events to avoid appearing confused on the witness stand. Preparing for trial is like preparing for an exam; studying her earlier statement is an important way to avoid inconsistencies in the testimony.

- Another way to help her recall significant details is by accompanying her to the scene of the crime, *if she agrees*. Because of the potentially disturbing nature of such a visit, she alone should make this decision. However, visiting the physical location will help her describe it in court and may stimulate her recollection in other important ways. In addition, a visit to the crime scene may occur in the process of the trial anyway; if so, a prior visit with you will help.

- To familiarize her with the setting, accompany her to the courtroom several days in advance of the trial. Pay special attention to the position of the witness stand and the direction she will face when giving testimony. If possible, it may be that you, a counselor, or a trusted family member could sit in public seating located directly in her line of vision from the witness stand. If she has a sympathetic face to look upon while testifying, rather than the defense attorney or assailant, it may help to ease her tension.

- Because she has to describe in detail what transpired during the rape, she needs to be comfortable with appropriate terminology to describe sex acts. This will help her avoid the use of "slang" terms which may discredit her.

- Double check with friends or other witnesses who have been subpoenaed to testify at the trial. Make sure they are aware of the correct time and location of the trial, and if necessary, help them arrange transportation or baby sitting.

- If the defense attorney asks to talk to her, she is under no legal obligation to do so and may refuse. Likewise, if she or those close to her receive threatening communications from the family or friends of the rapist, the district attorney should be informed. She is entitled to have the district attorney protect her from such harassment.

- Finally, make sure she is mentally prepared for the possibility of last minute delays or for a plea bargain before the case goes to trial. If it is clear that the victim is determined to stick with the case despite various delay tactics, many assailants will plead guilty to a lesser charge (e.g., attempted rape) in order to avoid the possibility of a longer sentence. Although the decision to accept a plea of guilty to reduced charges is made by the district attorney, at least it has the benefit of sparing her the ordeal of a trial. You may request that any decisions made by the district attorney should involve prior consultation with her.

Many women find the rape trial to be a negative experience, though for some it is therapeutic. Usually the most difficult aspect of the trial is the fact that the woman is called upon to publicly testify. This means that she must reveal the details of her rape to a group of strangers and be subject to cross examination by an attorney who will attempt to attack her character and question her version of events. Frequently the defense attorney will ask leading questions that imply a history of sexual promiscuity. Some victims feel that it is they who are on trial, not the assailant. Many states now have laws (often referred to as "rape shield laws") that limit questioning about the victim's sexual history. However, information about past sexual relations between the victim and the accused is admissible.

Finally, the trial itself is usually the first time the victim must confront her assailant face-to-face. In a very real sense, she is alone in front of a crowd, speaking publicly of a deeply private and humiliating experience. Without the support and understanding of you and others close to her, the courtroom experience threatens to further traumatize her and undermine her feeling of self-reliance.

GIVING TESTIMONY

During the trial, the defense attorney is likely to defend the rapist using one of three arguments.

1. The rape never took place and the story was invented by the woman in order to seek revenge or simply call attention to herself.

2. The rape did take place but the defendant was mistakenly identified as the assailant.

3. The woman was not a victim of rape but a willing participant in sexual intercourse.

Regardless of the approach taken by the defense, the victim usually has her character and judgment called into question during the cross-examination. The defense attorney may claim that she was too hysterical to make positive identification; that she fabricated events to "get even" or because she wants others to think she is sexually attractive; that she is sexually promiscuous and would have intercourse with anyone; that her "misconduct" (e.g., drinking) precipitated the event; or any other argument that undermines her credibility as a witness. Remember that the role of the defense attorney is to create doubt in the minds of judge and jury, so both she and you should be prepared to encounter accusations about her character and stereotypes about how women should act in various situations.

In order to prepare her to present testimony (or prepare you if you are a witness), there are several points to keep in mind.

- If possible, answer all questions directly without appearing uncertain. Statements such as "I don't know" or "I'm not sure" tend to raise doubts among the judge and jury.

- Be prepared for interruptions while giving testimony. People may wander in and out of court or the attorney may request a recess even though the testimony is in progress.

- While testifying, it is helpful to speak in a clear and deliberate manner. Take your time before responding to questions and maintain eye contact

with others in the room rather than staring at the
floor.

• Being properly dressed and well-groomed
enhances the credibility of the witness. Do not
wear blue jeans, shorts, T-shirt or tennis shoes to
the courtroom. Do not chew gum; the judge or
jury might find it distracting.

AFTER THE TRIAL

Despite the difficulties of a rape trial, hopefully there
is an important consolation—the conviction of the victim's
assailant. At the very least, the trial provides the victim with
an opportunity to express her anger toward the rapist and
feel a degree of justice being served. During and after the
trial, it is important to convey to her that she is not "changed"
in your eyes and in no way should she feel guilty for what
happened in the courtroom. Because cross-examination tends
to promote feelings of self-doubt, inadequacy, and confusion,
it is especially important that you reassure her of your
continued faith in her judgment and character. Many
victims emerge from a rape trial with anger and resentment
toward a legal system that seems to "protect the criminal and
condemn the victim." A heightened sensitivity on your part
to the difficulties of a rape trial is a great asset in
maintaining a positive relationship.

Given the nature of rape cases, there is a distinct
possibility that the offender will go free. If this occurs, under
no circumstances should you or others close to the victim
attempt to take justice into your own hands. Rather, there is
one other legal avenue that the victim can pursue. Although
most victims are not aware of this option, she has the right to
sue the rapist for damages. Such action would be a *civil* case
rather than a criminal one.

In a civil action, the burden of proof ("preponderance of evidence") is somewhat less stringent than is required in a criminal trial ("beyond a reasonable doubt"), and it is necessary only to establish that the victim suffered harm as a result of the defendant's action. Also, a unanimous jury verdict is not required for the victim to win a judgment, and it is possible also to sue third parties (e.g., fraternities, businesses) who should have anticipated and attempted to prevent the rape.

Of course, a successful civil action will not put the rapist in jail, and the victim is responsible for retaining a lawyer and absorbing legal fees. Nevertheless, such actions may help deter rape, and the monetary award can help compensate for lost wages.

Once legal action has been completed, it is helpful to discuss with her the likelihood of future contacts with the rapist. Working together to determine ways of coping with or avoiding such encounters may help reduce anxiety. For example, you have the right to request notification of when a convicted rapist will be released from prison. In addition, you must both be aware that the successful completion of legal action will not "make everything right." For one thing, if the rapist appeals the conviction, it may result in a second trial which again requires her to be a witness.

Much of the fear, anger and hurt could continue to persist after the trial. She may even feel responsible for the fact that a man was sent to prison, even though he was found guilty. Simply remind her that the judge and jury determined his fate, not she. Moreover, many rapists have committed *multiple* offenses and her courageousness in going to trial may save other women from a similar ordeal.

VICTIM ASSISTANCE PROGRAMS

In recent years, many states have passed legislation mandating a variety of benefits and services to assist victims of violent crime. Because these programs vary considerably from one state to another, only a very general summary can be given here. Your local police department and rape crisis center can provide you with details on the services available in your state.

The benefits and services may include:

- Financial compensation provided by the state and monetary restitution from the offender;

- Victim/witness assistance services, which include programs designed to keep the victim apprised of possible plea bargaining negotiations, pretrial release, and scheduling of sentencing and parole hearings. Also, some states allow for the introduction of "victim impact statements" at pre-sentence hearings. These statements detail medical, financial, and psychological damage caused by the crime, including changes in the victim's family relationships.

- Finally, several states have passed a "victim's bill of rights," which may require, among other things, that victims be made aware of the programs and services described above, notified of all court proceedings, provided with childcare and other social services (if needed), and protected against intimidation by the accused or his family and friends.

The effectiveness of these programs and services has not been systematically evaluated. However, the fact that they exist is evidence of increased sensitivity to the plight of violent crime victims in this country. It is also noteworthy that police training in most areas now pays special attention to the needs of rape victims. While seeking legal action against a rapist may be a difficult ordeal, the overall climate regarding the treatment of rape cases appears to be improving for victims.

10
Protecting Against Rape

Once a woman has been raped, it is common for her to experience prolonged and deep-seated fears concerning her safety. Unless one has had the experience of being the victim of criminal assault, it is difficult to understand why others who have been victims appear to be preoccupied with personal safety. Given the suddenness and extreme violence of rape, it is understandable for victims to feel an enduring sense of uneasiness or tension about everyday events that others take for granted. Fear of strangers, fear of going out of the house, fear of dating, and fear of being alone are just a few examples. It is important for you to realize that fears concerning personal safety, although seemingly "silly" or "unreasonable" from an outsider's standpoint, are rational and understandable from the victim's point of view. Furthermore, her state of mind is not likely to change simply because family or friends tell her that her fears are "ridiculous."

For both stranger and acquaintance rape situations, overt physical resistance to an attack may help or may further endanger the victim. Some claim that proficiency in self-defense techniques can provide an additional measure of safety. Others suggest that passive resistance, ranging from gentle persuasion to acting hysterically, may dissuade an assailant. The simple fact is that no one can say what is *always* the best response to an attack. Characteristics of the assailant and the circumstances will vary. All one can say with certainty is that anything which helps the victim to survive an attack is the right thing to do.

PREVENTING STRANGER RAPE

While it is true that there is no foolproof means to prevent future assaults, there are some steps to be taken which may ease a rape victim's fears and enhance her safety. The following represents a list of do's and don'ts which both you and she can take into account as a means of avoiding rape situations. This list has been compiled from a variety of lists suggesting protective measures against rape.

- Make sure her home is safe with deadbolt locks on doors, peep-hole viewer and window locks. Change the locks when moving to a new residence.

- If a stranger should come to the door, do not allow him in or indicate that no one else is home. Ask delivery or service persons for identification and do not allow children to ask strangers into the house. Make phone calls for strangers when there is an emergency. If a woman is alone in the house, she should pretend there is someone else home when a stranger visits.

- Women living alone should not list the first name on mail boxes or in telephone directories. In apartment complexes, women should avoid remaining alone in laundry rooms, basements, or garages. Make sure the entrance to the house is well-lighted.

- Always keep car doors locked, including when driving, and park in lighted areas. Before getting into a car, check the back seat. If there is car trouble, open the hood, attach a white cloth to the door and remain inside the locked car. If followed in a car by a stranger, drive directly to the police station.

- If one cannot avoid being alone on the street or a college campus late at night, stay in areas which are lighted and carry a police whistle. Try to avoid walking in places with dense woods or shrubs which could hide an assailant. Never hitchhike!

PREVENTING ACQUAINTANCE RAPE

Because acquaintance rape occurs most frequently in the context of adolescent dating relationships, efforts to prevent its occurrence require some understanding of the complexities of teen dating. As noted earlier, many fathers (and mothers) have a difficult time discussing dating with their daughters, and may resort instead to restrictions on her behavior (e.g., "grounding") to protect her from rape. Such actions are *not* recommended, as they do not help her develop the skills she needs to assess and avoid problem situations. Moreover, such actions are likely to produce conflict and poor communication between the two of you.

According to Ms. Py Bateman, Executive Director of **Alternatives to Fear,** which conducts workshops on acquaintance rape prevention and publishes a number of excellent materials for teens and their parents (see Resources):

1.   There must be trust and a pattern of open communication between you;

2.   You must be available to her as a resource and, if something seems to be bothering her, willing to try to open the discussion with her; and

3.   You must be careful to balance this notion of initiating discussion with the need to respect her privacy.   Regardless of how good your relationship with her is, she will probably have a difficult time discussing issues of sexuality and intimacy with you.

One way of discussing acquaintance rape prevention with your daughter in a manner which is less threatening is to focus instead on ways of developing and maintaining healthy dating relationships. For example:

•   It is perfectly acceptable to refuse a date and not feel guilty for doing so. It is a mistake to go out with someone out of guilt or because of peer pressure.

•   Males who act "macho" to secure dates should be avoided.   Observing such displays in possible dating partners can be a signal of potential future problems.

•   Don't be afraid to communicate limits concerning the desired degree of physical contact. No one has the right to force or manipulate another into undesired sexual acts, and it is important to learn to say no. Do not hesitate to let another know when touch makes you feel afraid, confused, guilty or manipulated. It is your right to set limits when physical contact makes you feel uncomfortable.

- Relationships that evolve gradually may be safer and more stable than "whirlwind romances." It is desirable to get to know another better before becoming emotionally and physically committed. A successful relationship is more likely if it develops gradually out of a sincere friendship.

- Relationships change. Assure your daughter that she has the right to end a relationship that is no longer healthy or fulfilling.

- Perhaps most important of all, remind her that healthy dating relationships are based on equality. The most successful relationships are those where partners share equally in the privileges and responsibilities of the relationship.

Finally, because acquaintance rape occurs most frequently in the context of dating relationships, which in turn revolve around the school setting, schools have become a focal point for prevention efforts. You can become involved in such efforts by finding out if the schools in your area present acquaintance rape prevention information. If they do not, encourage them to consider one of the currently available programs, such as the National Assault Prevention Center's TeenCap program (see Resources).

INVOLVEMENT WITH THE COMMUNITY

As we have indicated throughout this book, the experience of having a loved one endure the trauma of rape is likely to elicit powerful emotions in you: anger, sympathy, frustration, shame, grief and futility, to mention a few. While such feelings are understandable, we have emphasized that your primary concern should be directed toward the recovery of the woman. Do not hesitate to take advantage of agency services available in your community which offer counseling for rape victims and their loved ones.

It is possible for you to "work through" some of your feelings, especially feelings of futility, by taking constructive action to help both actual and potential rape victims. Working as a volunteer with various citizen action groups can channel your energies in a positive manner. For example, you might assist other rape victims and help to reduce the incidence of rape by serving as a volunteer in the following areas:

- helping with support services for rape victims (e.g., working the 24 hour crisis hotline);

- raising public consciousness about rape (e.g., distributing rape-related literature, helping sponsor community forums and workshops on rape, etc.);

- working to bring about legal reform (e.g., writing letters to state representatives concerning rape legislation, examining police and medical procedures for rape victims, etc.).

In many communities, rape crisis centers have been established and are already working in these and related areas. Serving as a volunteer in one of these agencies can be both a constructive outlet for your feelings and provide a badly needed service to others. At the very least, you may wish to contact the organizations listed in the appendix and ask for further information about how you can become involved.

11
Getting Help

Throughout this book, we have emphasized what husbands, fathers and male friends should and should not do in order to help rape victims recover. Because such a heavy demand is placed on these males to be supportive, they too are likely to need assistance. Helping these males is critical to helping victims.

In each community, there are likely to be a number of possible sources of help. Community mental health centers, pastoral counseling services, and private practitioners are but a few possibilities. There are also a number of national organizations dedicated to helping victims and their families (see Resources). In addition, over the past decade, hundreds of rape crisis centers have been established in communities throughout the United States and Canada. These centers specialize in addressing the unique personal and legal needs of victims. In every state and in nearly all large and medium size cities, these centers provide assistance to victims free of charge.

Despite the value of the services offered, our research indicates that relatively few husbands, fathers and male friends of rape victims seek assistance at these centers. Because we believe that rape crisis centers offer valuable help, it is important to examine some of the reasons why males may not use the service.

- Many males mistakenly believe that rape crisis centers are places only for women. Unfortunately, this misconception is reinforced by those who refer to these places as "women's centers." A more appropriate term would be "recovery centers" because in most instances, services are available to both men and women as they strive to deal with the aftermath of sexual assault.

- Another reason why males may not seek help at rape crisis centers is based on their beliefs about the staff who run these centers. It is true that the majority of staff at rape crisis centers are female. Because the issue of rape has been identified with the feminist movement, some males are likely to believe that they would be unwelcome intruders at rape crisis centers. They may believe that they would encounter hostility, or at the very least, the female staff would not be understanding or sympathetic to their concerns. In reality, many males who use rape crisis center services find a positive reception and a willingness by staff to provide them with help.

- Just as males should not assume that they are the "enemy" at rape crisis centers, neither should they believe that only another woman can truly understand what a rape survivor is going through.

Not only is it a myth to believe that rape is a "woman's problem," it is also a myth that only women can help other women who have been raped. Unfortunately, some males may get this impression by virtue of the fact that the staff is likely to be predominantly female.

- Perhaps one of the most significant reasons why males may not seek help at rape crisis centers is the *appearance* that the services are directed exclusively toward females. It is true that short term crisis counseling, as well as medical and legal assistance, tend to be organized around her immediate needs. However, some centers run groups for males, and offer individual short-term counseling to them. Virtually all centers can make referrals to help males locate services which are not available at the center.

Finally, as we have suggested earlier, many males are reluctant to seek help because they believe that needing assistance is a sign of weakness. We believe it is especially difficult for males in our culture to be open about their emotional vulnerabilities. Males need to understand that getting help is not a symptom of weakness or an admission that they "can't take it." Rather, it is a realization that there are those whose professional training places them in a position to offer useful advice at a time of great need. Seeking help at a rape crisis center or elsewhere is thus a way to gain strength and to preserve a relationship with a loved one.

12
A Final Note

We wish to stress once again that *you* can play a major role in helping a loved one recover from rape. However, there are no miracle cures and it is not likely that you alone can immediately "make everything right." By realizing that through sympathetic understanding you will exert a positive but necessarily limited influence, you can avoid the tendency to take personal responsibility for her ultimate happiness. By being patient, supportive, and non-judgmental toward her you will be communicating the most important message—your unconditional love. Finally, trust that she is strong enough to do the rest on her own.

Appendix A
Illustrative Case Studies*

While there are many possible reactions to the rape of a loved one, the following case studies will help you to understand proper and improper responses. These case studies illustrate many of the things one should and should not do when dealing with a rape victim. The most important point to remember is that the husbands, fathers and male friends of rape victims can be helpful or they can be harmful. With patience and understanding, men can minimize the terror and degradation experienced by women who have been raped.

CASE STUDY 1
Wendy: A Teenage Victim

The Incident

Wendy, a fourteen year old girl, was spending a few days with her girlfriend Betsy and Betsy's family at their

---

*Despite alterations, the names and situations in these illustrative case studies are substantively accurate and respresent real experiences.

summer cottage. One afternoon Wendy and Mark, Betsy's 16 year old brother, paddled the canoe to the far end of the lake—a heavily wooded area where there were no other cottages. Mark told Wendy that he had a bottle of wine and asked her if she would like to sit on the bank and drink with him. Always a rather adventuresome child, Wendy agreed to Mark's suggestion.

Although Mark drank the lion's share of wine, Wendy had a sufficient amount to feel light-headed and rather silly. Perhaps mistaking her elevated spirits as an indication of flirtatiousness, Mark put his arm around Wendy and began to kiss her on the lips. This was the first time Wendy had ever been kissed and, being rather taken back, she literally did not know how to respond. What's more, Mark did not stop at that point but aggressively began petting her. This frightened Wendy, but her inexperience in these matters caused her to be passive and not say anything. Suddenly Mark removed his bathing suit and told Wendy to do likewise. Frightened and confused, Wendy said she wanted to go back to the cottage. With a forceful tone, Mark said everything would be "all right" and that there was nothing for her to fear. In a rapid series of moves, he pulled off the bottom of Wendy's suit, pushed her on her back and entered her. In a state of shock, fear, confusion and physical pain, Wendy could only cry.

Although the entire episode lasted a few minutes, Wendy continued to cry for a long time. Her emotional state began to frighten Mark. Through her tears, Wendy managed to say "Why did you do that? You shouldn't have done that to me!" Mark clearly was scared. He tried to console her by indicating that it was only normal for people who liked each other to "make love." Then he said, "Besides, you should have said something earlier if you really didn't want to."

After returning to the cottage Wendy said nothing to Betsy or to the parents. In fact, Wendy said nothing to her own parents after she returned home. However, her emotional state and her behavior were definitely altered. Wendy was not clear as to her responsibility in the matter. She was certain that her parents would be angry with her if they knew she had been drinking. Even though her parents noticed that Wendy appeared to be moody and uncommunicative, they assumed it was merely a "phase."

Shortly after the new school year began, Wendy became ill at school for several consecutive days. Upon recommendation from the school nurse, Wendy received a medical exam which revealed that she was pregnant. Neither she nor her parents had suspected her condition.

Others React

The revelation of Wendy's pregnancy produced extreme anger in her parents, particularly her father. He could barely contain himself as he screamed his demands that she explain herself. Because Wendy had never communicated about sexual matters with her parents, she found it extremely difficult to discuss the event, especially with her father. Her understandable reluctance only served to escalate his anger to a point where he threatened to kick her out of the house. Finally, she broke down in fits of weeping and managed to describe what had happened.

Wendy gave an honest account to her parents, though her inexperience in the area of sexuality deeply embarrassed her and compounded her difficulties in communicating. Wendy had many unanswered questions in her own mind, but the anger of her parents made it difficult for her to share those questions and receive feedback. She had questions about her own sexuality, about the nature of pregnancy, about whether others blamed her, and about what would happen to her friendship with Betsy and other peers. In addition, Wendy had great concern over what should be done with the baby and whether or not she would be able to finish school. The anger and shame of her parents only added to the depression Wendy was feeling.

Without asking Wendy's opinion, her parents decided to send her away to a special school for the duration of her pregnancy. When the child was born, it would be placed for adoption without Wendy ever seeing it. In addition, her father sought legal action against Mark and his parents on a wide variety of charges. Again, this action was taken without consulting Wendy. Furthermore, Wendy was denied the right to see her group of friends. Her every move was carefully scrutinized by her father. Finally, Wendy's entire family engaged in a "conspiracy of silence" wherein her "encounter" (they avoided using the word rape) and subsequent condition were never mentioned by anyone.

Although Wendy's parents meant well, her feelings about what was happening seemed to be of secondary importance to the feelings and wishes of her mother and father. It was clear that her parents, especially her father—whose will usually prevailed in family matters—were embarrassed by the situation. They tended to blame Wendy for poor judgment. Even though Wendy received proper medical attention, her parents never sought to provide her with counseling. In a state of utter depression, feeling isolated, insecure and guilty, Wendy attempted to take her life. Although she survived the attempt, her physical and mental state were such that she had to be hospitalized for a lengthy period of time.

In the spring, Wendy gave birth to a baby girl whom she never saw. Although that was several years ago, the impact of those events is still very much evident in her life. Wendy has continued to receive professional help but her emotional recovery has been slow and very painful.

Lessons to be Learned

In a sense, Wendy became a multiple victim of a single crime. She was victimized not only by rape, but also by an unwanted pregnancy and a lack of understanding in the home. Unfortunately, her situation is similar to that of many teenagers who have been raped.

In almost every instance, the reactions of her parents, especially her father, compounded Wendy's emotional trauma. Rather than communicating unconditional love and support, Wendy's parents communicated anger and embarrassment.

When Wendy's parents learned of her rape and pregnancy, a calm and understanding approach was in order. The anger and threats of her parents made it difficult for Wendy to express her feelings. She was being blamed for poor judgment and lack of character when in fact, her only "fault" was a lack of understanding and experience in sexual matters. Unfortunately, Wendy was never provided with an appropriate resource person with whom she could have frank discussions about sexuality and pregnancy. In the absence of information, Wendy's fears continued to grow.

At every phase in the decision making process, Wendy should have been given the opportunity to share her feelings. Decisions affecting her should not have been made without her input. This is especially true in respect to the decisions made for her about her schooling and her baby.

Wendy's parents also made the mistake of isolating her from her network of friends at a time when she most needed them. Limiting contact with her peers (including her friend Betsy) reflected her parents' shame rather than an awareness of Wendy's needs. Concern over the family reputation seemed to be more important than addressing Wendy's emotional needs. Finally, the "conspiracy of silence" prevailing in the home communicated to Wendy that her behavior was too terrible even to be discussed. Feeling guilty, confused, isolated and unable to communicate with those persons she loved most, it is not surprising that Wendy's depression led to an attempted suicide.

What Wendy's Parents Should Have Done

- **Wendy's parents should have responded to her need for unconditional love.** Parents who spend time blaming others or themselves for the rape of their child waste valuable time and energy. This energy should be directed toward reassuring and supporting the victim.

- **Wendy's parents should have let her know that someone would be willing to talk to her about adult intimacy.** Since the rape was Wendy's first sexual experience, Wendy needed reassurance that her fears and questions about adult intimacy could be discussed. Such a discussion with either her parents, a trusted adult, or a counselor, would have helped Wendy realize that her capacity for sexual intimacy in adulthood had not been diminished.

● **Wendy's parents should have arranged for professional assistance to help the family communicate more effectively.** Unfortunately, counseling to help Wendy deal with the rape, her pregnancy, and her parents' reactions was not provided until after Wendy's attempted suicide. Early professional assistance would have improved the communication between Wendy and her parents. Communication between parents and adolescents is often strained even under normal conditions. During the crisis produced by rape, effective communication is made even more difficult. Improved communication, paired with greater understanding and support at home, would have spared Wendy and her family a great deal of unnecessary pain.

● **Wendy's parents should have allowed Wendy to return to her normal activities.** By encouraging Wendy to resume her normal lifestyle as much as possible, her parents would have provided her with a much needed sense of normalcy. It also would have increased Wendy's access to her friends and peers who could have provided important support.

● **Wendy's parents should have been more considerate of her rights and feelings.** Such consideration would have helped Wendy to not feel punished and excluded. When Wendy's parents refused to discuss with her the rape experience and her future, they communicated

that they were ashamed of her and that they held
her responsible for being assaulted. Had Wendy's
parents listened to her and included her in the
decision making process, she would not have felt
so isolated and could have taken an active role in
her recovery process.

CASE STUDY 2
Carla: A Case of Acquaintance Rape

The Incident

Carla is twenty-eight years old, single, and teaches
elementary school in a suburban community.   While
returning to her apartment from a dance class one evening,
she was approached in the parking lot by her former
boyfriend, Ron. Although they had stopped dating—by
mutual agreement—nearly a year ago, Ron still called her
from time to time. Carla sensed that he had never totally
accepted the fact that their relationship was over. On this
occasion Ron seemed distraught. Even though she could
smell alcohol on his breath, Carla agreed to let him come
inside and talk about what was troubling him.

Once they were inside her apartment, there was an
abrupt change in Ron's mood. He became very belligerent
and aggressive. He told Carla that even though she was now
dating another man, she would always be his girl. Carla
could tell by now that Ron had been drinking heavily. She
became concerned for her safety.   She recalled two
occasions during their dating relationship when Ron was
physically abusive to her after he had been drinking. She
tried to calm him down and offered to make coffee, but Ron
was too drunk and angry to listen to reason. He told her that
he thought it would be the "right thing" for them to make

love. Carla strongly refused. He then slapped her and forced her into the bedroom where he raped her. Afterwards, he warned her not to say anything to anyone and joked that even if she did, no one would believe her anyway.

As soon as he left, Carla composed herself somewhat and tried to decide what to do. Should she report the rape to the police? If she did report it, would the police believe her? After nearly an hour of soul-searching, she decided to call her boyfriend, Dale. She was confident that Dale would believe her and would help her decide on the right course of action.

Others React

Dale arrived within fifteen minutes and Carla, though considerably upset, told him what had happened. Dale was shocked and confused by her story. He wanted to ask her what she was doing with Ron in the first place and why he was in her apartment. However, he realized that Carla needed support and advice, not questions. Although Dale said it was her decision, he advised her to report the assault to the police. Even though the police might question a charge of rape against a former boyfriend, Dale felt that Carla would have to bring charges against Ron or run the risk of being raped again. Carla agreed. Within two days, Ron was arrested and charged with rape. Shortly thereafter, he was indicted at a preliminary hearing and a trial date was set.

Meanwhile, Carla returned to work after a week's leave of absence. She and Dale tried to resume their normal pattern of social activities. Privately, though, Dale was having doubts. Carla had told him several times that her relationship with Ron was over. However, she had said also that Ron called her occasionally to "talk about old times." In addition, a mutual friend of Ron and Carla's told Dale that she had known Ron for several years and found it difficult to believe he would force himself on Carla. Ron, for his part, was strongly denying that he had raped Carla, even though he admitted to having sexual relations with her that night. After all, he reasoned, they had virtually lived together at one time and had continued to maintain regular contact with one another.

Dale felt guilty for doubting Carla's version of events, but the doubts would not go away. At the same time, they stopped socializing with many of their friends because a number of them were also friends of Ron. Several mutual friends had hinted that Carla probably agreed to have sexual relations with Ron, later calling it rape to preserve her relationship with Dale. As the strain on their relationship grew, Carla and Dale argued more frequently and were no longer able to communicate openly with each other. Finally, Dale confronted her with his suspicions that she had fabricated the rape charge to cover up her own promiscuity. Carla wanted to prove to Dale that his suspicions were unfounded. However, his unwillingness to trust and support her convinced her that it was not worth the effort. She thus became increasingly isolated from Dale and her friends.

To make matters worse, the district attorney decided that there was not sufficient evidence to yield a conviction. As a result, the case was dropped. In Dale's mind, this confirmed his worst suspicions about Carla's fidelity and honesty. No longer able to effectively communicate, Dale and Carla ended their relationship. Since then Carla has lost contact with a number of her former friends and has found it increasingly difficult to resume dating other men.

Lessons to be Learned

The impact of Carla's rape on her relationship with her male friend, Dale, is similar to that of many other cases of acquaintance rape. Initially, Dale appeared supportive and understanding. He did not pressure Carla with questions but rather attempted to do what was best for her. However, Dale's ability to be supportive gradually eroded in the face of his doubts about her honesty and fidelity. In attending to the comments of their mutual friends, Dale allowed casual gossip to cloud his trust of Carla. He therefore jeopardized their ability to communicate. Dale could have been more helpful to Carla and himself if he had approached the situation differently.

What Dale Should Have Done

- **Dale should have applauded Carla's willingness to help a friend in distress (even if that friend was a former lover).** Instead of communicating doubts about her honesty, he should have demonstrated his trust in Carla and his love for her by not letting his anger dominate their relationship. Had Dale realized the trust Carla had placed in him by confiding in him, he may not have doubted her fidelity.

- **Dale should not have been influenced by gossip.** Allowing the gossip of associates to influence his decision only worked to the disadvantage of preserving his relationship with Carla. It would have been much better if Dale had stood by Carla to help her fend off rumors, rather than abandoning her at the time of her greatest need.

- **Dale should have considered professional counseling.** A professional counselor could have helped Dale realize that the expression of friendship which Carla extended to Ron did not imply any desire for sexual intimacy. Through counseling, Dale would have learned to reassure Carla that she was in no way responsible for Ron's sexual assault upon her.

CASE STUDY 3
Lisa: Rape Victim with Nonsupportive Partner

The Incident

At approximately 3:00 a.m. on a hot summer night, Lisa was awakened from a sound sleep by the presence of someone in her bedroom. At first she thought it was her four year old son Tommy, but an instant later she was frozen in terror when the figure of a man hovered over her and said, "Bitch, I'm gonna rape you; if you scream, I'll go after your kid." Lisa's terror was so complete that she could neither speak nor move. She was engulfed in a sensation of "unreality," almost as if she were watching a movie rather than being the victim of a horrifying event. As the man began to remove her bed clothing, Lisa's immediate concern was for the safety of her son and so she did not fight her assailant.

As the stranger descended upon her, Lisa managed to say, "Please! Please don't!" In a half mocking, half vengeful voice the man replied, "I've been watching you and I think you're gonna like this." Reeking of alcohol and whispering profanities in her ear, the man proceeded to rape her. The room was dark and Lisa never saw his face. After ten minutes, which seemed like an eternity, the stranger started to leave. He turned back to Lisa, "If you try calling the police, I'll be back. This is between you and me — if I have to come back, you and your kid won't be so lucky next time." With those words, the rapist bolted through an open window into the night. Lisa ran into Tommy's room, saw that he was undisturbed, and then sat down trembling and weeping.

Lisa did not go to the police. She did not speak of the incident to anyone. Rather, she waited for her husband Barry, who would return in two weeks from his current tour of duty in the Navy. Those two weeks were filled with fear for herself and her son. She had a great deal of self-doubt as to whether she had done the right thing, as well as considerable apprehension over how her husband would respond. Lisa knew that her rape was going to complicate an already stressful situation.

Others React

When her husband Barry finally returned home, he sensed almost immediately that Lisa was behaving in an unusual way. He asked her what was wrong. Not wanting to spoil Barry's homecoming, she claimed that everything was fine. However, her expression betrayed her words. Barry, never a particularly patient man, began to lose his temper and insisted that she tell him about the problem. Lisa could contain her tears no longer and blurted out that she had been raped.

Barry sat in stunned silence as Lisa recounted the event. He did not interrupt her but he clearly was becoming angry. When she finished, he said, "If I catch the b......, I'm going to kill him!" He told her that she shouldn't worry because he'd find a way to "get" the guy. He then proceeded to ask Lisa for information that would help him identify the rapist. "What did he look like?" "How tall was he?" "How old did he seem?" "What was he wearing?" "What did his voice sound like?" When Lisa claimed that she had no idea who the man was and appeared unable to provide Barry with answers, he became very annoyed with her and implied that she was being uncooperative. He never asked if she had seen a doctor of if she needed someone to talk to about the incident.

During the next several days, Barry appeared to be preoccupied with the rape and talked of it constantly. Not only was he deeply angered, he was also beginning to have doubts about Lisa's role in her victimization. He began to ask her questions such as, "Why didn't you lock the window?" "Why didn't you fight him?" "What do you think you did to make him pick you?" "Why did you decide not to call the police?" "Are you sure you don't have any idea who the guy is?" Even though this type of questioning upset Lisa very much, her husband seemed unable to contain his anger or doubts. He continued to make her discuss the incident.

Other aspects of their relationship also suffered. Barry spent little time with their son, preferring instead to be at the tavern "thinking." In terms of their sexual relationship, Lisa was confused and upset by what happened to her; she simply could not respond to Barry's advances. At first he appeared to be understanding and did not force the issue. Then one night after he had been drinking, Barry insisted that she "stop acting like a child and start acting like a wife." When Lisa apologized but still remained reluctant, Barry became abusive. He pushed her down and screamed at her, "If you can do it with him, you can do it with me!" Never did Lisa feel more alone than at that moment.

Barry was home for approximately six weeks before his next tour of duty. All the problems that existed in their marriage before Lisa's rape were exaggerated and brought out into the open. By the end of his stay, it was apparent that their marriage was in serious trouble. Lisa became aware of a fundamental failure in communication. She felt that Barry had abandoned her emotionally when she most needed him. For his part, the rape enhanced Barry's suspicions about Lisa's faithfulness. He could not understand why she seemed so cold and distant. In a way, the anger that each felt toward the rapist shifted toward the other person.

After Barry departed, Lisa and her son moved back to her parent's house. She is currently seeking the assistance of a counselor and is undecided about whether she is committed to continuing her marriage with Barry.

Lessons to be Learned

It is clear from Lisa's case that her husband's anger and distrust blinded Barry to her condition and to the problems she was facing. His initial preoccupation with revenge and his doubts about Lisa's judgment and fidelity only heightened her distress. Barry's drinking, his anger toward Lisa, and his premature demands that she be sexually responsive to his needs put severe strains upon their relationship. This prolonged her recovery and undermined the probabilities that their marriage would survive. It also reduced Barry's ability to function as a father, husband and lover. If Barry was to have played a positive role in Lisa's recovery, he should have acted much differently.

What Barry Should Have Done

- **Barry's first concern should have been Lisa's physical and mental welfare.** Barry should have insisted that his wife undergo a thorough medical examination. Not only would this have protected Lisa from disease and physical harm which may have resulted from the rape, it would also have been a demonstration of his love and support.

- **Barry should have put his anger and doubts aside, listened carefully to Lisa, and taken his cues from her.** Barry's quick interest in revenge was an indication that he was much more concerned with his own feelings than with those of his wife.

- **Barry should have refrained from "interrogating" Lisa.** In so doing, he would have greatly reduced her feelings of guilt and anxiety. Words of comfort and support were needed to assure Lisa that she was a victim; she was not in any way to blame for the rape.

- **Barry should have encouraged Lisa to seek the assistance of a counselor, perhaps at the nearest rape crisis center.** He should have also considered relationship counseling. Their marriage, which was in some jeopardy prior to the rape, was now in serious trouble. With professional help, communications between Barry and Lisa could have been improved.

- **Barry should not have intimidated Lisa into having sexual relations with him.** By so doing,

Barry demonstrated a lack of understanding and respect for the pain and terror Lisa experienced. His actions toward her communicated that he considered her to be a willing participant in a sexual act with a stranger—not a victim of violence. Barry should have realized that a woman who has been raped requires time to recover and to regain her normal desire for sexual intimacy. He should have been with Lisa to hold and comfort her—not to make sexual demands.

- **Barry should not have "abandoned" Lisa and their son.** In failing to spend time with his son, Barry placed the full responsibility of child care on Lisa. In addition, his absence from the home not only caused Lisa to worry, but also communicated his rejection of her and their son.

CASE STUDY 4
Barbara: Rape Complicated by Racial Prejudice

The Incident

Barbara is a white, forty-five year old housewife who resides in a large city on the east coast. She and her husband Paul, a bus driver for the city transit system, have three children. Barbara does her grocery shopping every Tuesday morning at the same local supermarket where she has shopped for 13 years.

On this particular Tuesday, Barbara left the store with two armloads of groceries and walked around the side of the building to her automobile. As she reached her car, two black men in their early twenties approached her and offered to help put the groceries in the trunk. Before she

could reply, one of the men pulled out a knife and placed it
to her throat while the other clamped a hand over her mouth
and spun her around by the arm. As the groceries scattered
in all directions, Barbara was dragged behind a dumpster
and gagged with her own scarf. It was broad daylight and
she could see houses across the street, but there were no
people in sight. She was raped repeatedly by the two men
and subjected to a stream of verbal abuse which left little
doubt as to how the men felt about white females.

When the ordeal was finally over, the two rapists
seemed surprisingly remorseful and were almost
considerate. They helped her to her feet, brushed the dirt
off her clothes, picked up the groceries on the ground beside
her car and tossed them into the back seat. As soon as she
was inside the car, she locked the doors and drove directly
home. Once inside the garage, she began weeping.

Others React

She was still crying fifteen minutes later when her
youngest son Tim, age fifteen, arrived home from school.
He wanted to know what had happened. She simply told
him to call the dispatcher at the transit company to request
that her husband Paul be sent straight home. By the time
Paul arrived, their daughter Karen, age 17, had also returned
home from school. Barbara sent the children out of the
room while she told the story to her husband. Paul called
the police, who suggested that he take Barbara to the
hospital immediately for an examination. Two uniformed
officers met them there to take a preliminary statement from
Barbara.

Before leaving for the hospital Paul told the children:
"Your mother has been raped by two black men. She's going

to be all right, but she needs some medical attention. Then she has to talk to the police. I'll call you from the hospital. In the meantime, call your older brother at work and tell him what's happened." With that, Paul and Barbara left for the hospital.

Blake, the eldest son, left work at the foundry when his brother called. He drove to his parent's house to await the call from his father. As might be expected, Blake's younger siblings looked to him for guidance. When his father called home to recount what had happened, Blake went into an angry tirade about black people and "other low lifes who should be shot." He was convinced that the police and courts would probably do nothing about the crime and that the only way to guarantee justice was to "take it into your own hands."

For weeks after the rape, there seemed to be little progress in apprehending the rapists. Both Paul and Blake continually discussed, in front of the rest of the family, their feelings about black people who "live off the sweat of others, commit all the crimes, and still go free." These frequent expressions of outrage were beginning to have a profound impact on the others. For example, Karen became very reluctant to talk to one of her fellow high school cheerleaders who was black. She also felt very uneasy about black males at school, even though she had been on good terms with them all during high school.

Tim was also influenced by the racial sentiments of his father and older brother. He began to notice things about the blacks at school that had never before drawn his attention. He avoided sitting near blacks on the school bus and in the cafeteria. He and his friends found themselves frequently discussing how black people were "different" and how they always seemed to be the trouble makers at school. One day Tim and his friends vandalized several lockers used by black students. This in turn heightened racial tensions at school and set off several other interracial incidents. Tim and the others were caught and had to pay for damages. They also spent considerable time in detention. Although Tim's actions were frowned upon by school officials, at home his father and brother treated him like a hero.

As a consequence, Barbara was deeply affected not only by her victimization, but also by the perpetual discussions about blacks. Instead of the tension in the home subsiding during the weeks following the rape, it grew worse. Barbara became increasingly fearful that members of her family would end up hurt or in jail. She was especially upset over what happened to Tim at school. When she discovered that Blake had purchased a gun and was keeping it in his car, she was at a total loss as to what she could do. Finally, in order to protect Blake from himself, she removed the weapon from his car and threw it in the river. This made both her husband and Blake angry with her. The rapists were never caught but the subject of race continues to be an issue of contention in Barbara's family.

Lessons to be Learned

Due to her family's preoccupation with "racial justice," Barbara's recovery needs were poorly attended. Barbara's need for emotional support was shoved aside because of emotionally charged racial prejudices. As a result, the family became divided rather than united. Under no circumstances should Paul and Blake have been angry with Barbara for her actions concerning the gun. They needed to realize that her motive was to protect Blake from physical harm and legal entanglements. When family members take matters into their own hands, it is likely that they will make matters worse. They may even become targets of the legal system. This is a sure way to complicate the recovery of a rape victim.

Paul and Blake's reactions to the rape had an equally troubling impact on the younger children. Constant racial slurs and an interpretation of the rape strictly on the basis of race, made the children unduly fearful and angry toward all blacks. A generalized anxiety toward an entire group of people, based upon the assumption that they are all basically alike, is highly debilitating and an impediment to daily functioning. In the case of Karen, her previously friendly relationships with blacks suffered. In addition, her fear toward black males was developing into an unhealthy preoccupation. Such feelings probably would not have emerged if Paul and Blake had responded differently.

Also tragic is what happened to Tim. His actions grew out of the strong pressure for revenge against blacks that he felt at home. Certainly his beliefs about black people were based on inaccurate assumptions and tended to reflect the perpetual tensions of his home life. His actions in vandalizing the lockers at school only functioned to identify him as a trouble maker in the eyes of authorities. This had serious negative consequences for his subsequent academic performance. Unfortunately, Tim's father and older brother reinforced the very behavior which hurt both him and his mother.

In the final analysis, Barbara's recovery was complicated and prolonged by the behavior of Paul and Blake. She was made to assume the added burden of worrying about their safety, as well as the disturbing behaviors of the children. The atmosphere in the home caused by her husband and her elder son made it difficult for the family to function effectively. They were all hurt.

What Paul and Blake Should Have Done

- **Paul and Blake should have focused their attention upon Barbara's needs.** They should have left the issue of justice to the authorities. Because Paul and Blake were so caught up in seeking revenge, they neglected to provide the love and support which a rape victim desperately needs.

- **Paul and Blake should have realized that all men of any race are not rapists.** They should have communicated this to Barbara and the children. Such a generalization was very unfair and intensified existing racial prejudices. It also increased the family's anxiety and disrupted their lives.

- **Paul and Blake should have channeled their energy toward assisting in Barbara's recovery.** They could have suggested professional counseling for Barbara. They could also have considered counseling for themselves to help them resolve their anger and frustration. This would have removed a large burden from Barbara, who became very concerned for her family's safety.

CASE STUDY 5
Lori: Rape Victim with Supportive Partner

The Incident

Lori is an attractive twenty-four year old woman who is employed as a distributor for a large textbook company. On an evening in March, Lori was returning to her apartment after a lengthy sales meeting. When she parked her car and opened the door a man appeared out of nowhere and grabbed her by the arm. He displayed a knife and forced her to drive with him to a deserted spot. He explained to her that they were going to "have some fun." If she screamed or in any way resisted, he would use the knife on her.

Although she did not suffer severe physical injury, Lori was subjected to extreme terror, vulgar language and degrading sexual acts. At no time during the rape did Lori feel she could effectively use force to resist the assault. However, she did plead with him (without success) to let her go. Even though the event seemed to her like a fragmented nightmare, Lori had the presence of mind to take mental notes that later proved helpful to the police. After the attack, despite the fact that she felt "filthy," she went directly to the police without bathing or changing clothing. Lori was aware of the importance of physical evidence and was determined to see the rapist punished.

Others React

After a brief preliminary report, Lori was taken directly to a hospital for examination and treatment. Up until this point, Lori had remained remarkably controlled. However, it was at the hospital that she began to show signs of the emotional strain. This stress was further compounded by the actions of those who were supposed to help her. Lori was made to wait in the emergency room in her disheveled condition for nearly one hour. She was then examined by a male doctor. He was professional in demeanor, but did not appear to be sensitive to her emotional state. The series of rape examination procedures, though routine to the doctor, were discomforting to Lori and added to her distress. During this time, she was deeply concerned about the potential responses of her family and of John, her fiance, who as yet had not been informed of what happened.

When the medical examination had been completed, Lori was taken home by a police officer and allowed to bathe and change clothing. It was requested that she return to the police station that evening to provide a full account of the event. While at home, Lori telephoned her fiance to briefly explain what happened. She asked him to meet her at the police station. Although John was very upset and wanted her to explain more fully what had happened, he agreed to meet her as requested.

When John arrived at the police station, Lori was being questioned by detectives. As he sat waiting for her, John felt angry, hurt, confused and highly apprehensive. He did not know what to expect. He was concerned about how this incident would change his relationship with Lori. As Lori emerged from the room where she was questioned, John held out his arms and they embraced without saying a word. Lori began to cry. Although John also felt like crying, he held her and told her how much he loved her. John wanted very much for Lori to tell him what happened, but he sensed that this was not the appropriate time for such a discussion.

When the police finished questioning her, John took Lori back to her apartment and offered to make her a hot meal. Although Lori seemed silent and distant, he realized that her silence was not an attempt to shut him out, but rather an understandable response to what had happened. It was then that John held her hand and said: "Look, I'm just as confused about this as you. I want to know what happened to you. However, I realize you may need some time to sort things out. Whenever you're ready, I'm willing to listen. I also want you to know that I don't blame you for what happened. You shouldn't blame yourself either. All that really matters is that you are OK; that we love each other. This is going to be hard on both of us but if we trust and help each other, I know we can get through it."

Lori was visibly relieved by what John said. However, she was very anxious about how her parents would react to news of the rape. John asked her if she would like him to break the news to her family. Together they discussed various approaches. Lori decided that John would tell her family and, when she was ready, they would both answer any questions her parents had.

In part, as a result of his support and the support of her family, Lori decided to press charges against the rapist. The case was scheduled for trial and John was understanding and supportive of Lori's decision to pursue legal action. John took time off from work to be with her during the trial. They were married that fall.

Lessons to be Learned

John's behavior throughout Lori's ordeal suggests a high level of emotional security and self-awareness. John had no difficulty in understanding that she was a victim and therefore not responsible for what happened. He did not question her judgment nor her inability to physically resist the assault. Although he did have questions about what happened to her, he did not pressure her into talking about the incident. He took his cues from her rather than imposing his will by making decisions for her. John showed great patience and sensitivity by giving Lori's immediate needs a higher priority than his own.

Of equal importance to Lori's recovery, John communicated in clear terms that he did not hold her responsible for what occurred. He let her know that his love for her was unchanged. John also let her know that he was willing to help her and stick by her throughout the legal process. John's assistance in approaching Lori's family demonstrated his support. In a way, Lori's victimization dramatically proved John's love and trust. Their relationship was actually strengthened by the experience. Lori, as a result, was able to reclaim her health much sooner than is typical for many women following the horrid crime of rape.

What John Did

John clearly was an important asset in Lori's recovery. Husbands, fathers and male friends have much to offer recovering rape victims if they follow John's example.

- **John placed Lori's needs ahead of his own.** Because Lori was not distracted by John's struggles, she focused her full attention on her own feelings and recovery.

- **John provided support but followed Lori's cues.** While he offered advice, he allowed Lori to make her own decisions.

- At no time did John suggest or imply that Lori was responsible for her victimization.

- John was helpful in communicating with Lori's family. By doing so, he served as a buffer and further demonstrated his support for Lori.

- John demonstrated his support for Lori by taking time off from work to be with her during the trial.

- Throughout the entire ordeal, John's presence and support assured Lori that she was not alone. This was his greatest contribution.

CASE STUDY 6
Ellen: Rape Victim with a Father Who Expressed His Anger Constructively

The Incident

It was Ellen's first visit to the large University attended by her older sister, Cynthia, and the directions to Cynthia's apartment — which Cynthia had dictated to her over the phone — were no help at all. Also, it was getting dark and the street signs were becoming more difficult to read. As she drove slowly along, looking for a phone booth, she saw two friendly-looking males standing next to their car. Given her proximity to the campus, she assumed that these males were students. Ellen stopped and asked them for directions to Cynthia's apartment. The men responded that they had a map in their car and she was welcome to look at it.

As she stood next to their car, studying the map in the deepening twilight, one of the men suddenly opened the back door of the car and the other man pushed her into it. Clamping his hand over her mouth to keep her from screaming, he whispered that if she kept quiet and cooperated, no harm would come to her. They then drove her to an apartment, where she was raped by both of them. Later, they dropped her off at a park several blocks from where her car was parked, and warned her: "Don't tell anyone about this. We have your driver's license, so we know where you live."

Still in a state of shock, Ellen nevertheless managed to get to a phone booth at a nearby convenience store and call Cynthia. Cynthia picked her up and drove her immediately to the university medical center emergency room. By the time the emergency room examination had been completed, Ellen had decided to go to the police station and file charges against her assailants. She did so and, later that night, she and Cynthia made a long distance call to their parents, Judy and Roger, to tell them what had happened. Roger had embarked recently on a second career as a counselor, and Ellen hoped that his newly-acquired crisis intervention skills would enable him to deal with what had happened.

Others React

Even though he knew that anger would not help his daughter recover, Roger was furious and could think of nothing but getting revenge against the "punks" who had violated Ellen. In a way, it was fortunate that Cynthia's apartment was a three hour drive from where they lived, because it gave Judy some time to help Roger vent his anger, *before* they met with Ellen. Judy, coincidentally, had been training as a volunteer at the local rape crisis center, and sooner than she expected, she was putting her training to use.

By the time they reached Cynthia's apartment, Roger had cooled down considerably. He hugged Ellen and told her that he loved her, that he and Judy were proud of her for having survived, and that they would be there to support her throughout the police investigation and subsequent trial.

On the way home, Judy told Roger that she was proud of *him*, too, for offering Ellen what she most needed. Roger confided that his intense hatred for the rapists had not gone away and wouldn't for a long time. To make matters worse, Ellen's case did not go to trial. Even though Ellen's case provided the prosecuting attorney with what Roger felt was clearcut evidence of rape, the grand jury decided not to hand down an indictment against the assailants.

Confused and bitter, Roger nevertheless decided that "I should use my anger to solve problems, rather than create them." The following week, he began training as a volunteer at the local rape crisis center, in part to come to grips with his own emotions over what had happened to Ellen, but also to help other men who were "secondary victims" of sexual assault. He quickly discovered, however, that this particular rape crisis center's services were designed (as they should be) to help the primary victim, and that they were not able to offer him much help. He would have to seek assistance elsewhere. Also, from his own experience as a counselor, he knew that males are much less likely than females to seek help from counselors or other mental health professionals.

It was then that Roger decided to start a support group for male "significant others" of rape victims. He solicited referrals from the rape crisis center, the police, and the local community mental health center, and held the meetings in his own home. To his dismay, attendance at the meetings was (and still is) sporadic. Furthermore, he found that even in his group meetings, which were designed to be as non-threatening as possible, many of the men were still unwilling to open up and talk about what they were feeling. Nevertheless, several of the men remarked to Roger that the sessions had helped them through some very difficult emotional crises. In fact, a number of the participants indicated that this group was the only place where they felt that their feelings were understood and accepted, and that they were now able to deal more effectively with what had happened. Also, Roger was at last free of his anger and, consequently, his relationship with Ellen was better than it had ever been before.

Lessons to be Learned

In some respects, Roger's behavior was atypical in that he was not only willing to seek professional assistance immediately, but he also created an opportunity for other males to have an outlet for their feelings. Although he felt the same emotions as any loving father would under the circumstances, he was able to find a helpful rather than harmful way to deal with those powerful feelings. His chief concern was the recovery of his daughter, rather than finding a means to seek revenge. In the end, he created a family climate where all could recover, and where relationships were strengthened rather than tested to the limit.

What Roger Did

- **Roger found a constructive way to deal with his anger.** At no time did Roger let his desire for revenge override his judgment as to what was best for his daughter. He maintained enough emotional control and let her needs dictate his actions.

- **Roger consistently communicated a message of love and support to his daughter and to other family members.** In this manner, he helped create a nurturing climate for the recovery of each family member.

- **Roger set an example not only for his family, but for other males who have experienced the rape of a loved one.** By creating a support group for secondary victims, Roger was able to constructively deal with his feelings and allow others to do likewise. This represented a service beyond price.

Appendix B
Suggested Readings

Adams, A. and Abarbanel, G. *Sexual Assault on Campus: What Colleges Can Do*. Santa Monica Hospital Rape Treatment Center, 1988.

Ageton, S.S. *Sexual Assault Among Adolescents*. MA: D.C. Health & Company, 1983.

Aizenman, M. and Kelley, G. "The Incidence of Violence and Acquaintance Rape in Dating Relationships Among College Men and Women." *Journal of College Student Development*, Vol. 29, No. 4, 305-311, 1988.

Amir, M. *Patterns in Forcible Rape*. Chicago: University of Chicago Press, 1971.

Bard, M., and Sangrey, D. *The Crime Victim's Book*. (2nd ed.), New York: Brunner/Mael Publishers, 1986.

Bart, P.B. and O'Brien, P.H. *Stopping Rape: Successful Survival Strategies*. NY: Pergamon Press, 1985.

Becker, J.V., et al. "Level of Postassault Sexual Functioning in Rape and Incest Victims." *Archives of Sexual Behavior,* Vol. 15, No. 1, 37-49, 1986.

Belk, S. and Snell, W. "Avoidance Strategy Use in Intitmate Relationships." *Journal of Social and Clinical Psychology,* Vol. 7, 80-96, 1988.

Benedict, H. *Recovery: How to Survive Sexual Assault for Women, Men, Teenagers, Their Friends and Families.* Garden City, NY: Doubleday & Company, 1985.

Benedict, H. *Safe, Strong, and Streetwise: Sexual Safety at Home, on the Street, on Dates, on the Job, at Parties, and More.* Little Brown, 1987.

Berger, R.J., et al. "Sexual Assault in a College Community." *Sociological Focus,* Vol. 19, No. 1, 1-26, 1986.

Bourque, L.B. *Defining Rape.* Durham: Duke University Press, 1989.

Bridges, J.S. and McGrail, C.A. "Attributions of Responsibility for Date and Stranger Rape." *Sex Roles,* Vol. 21, No. 3/4, 273-286, 1989.

Burgess, A.W. and Holmstrom, L.L. "Rape Trauma Syndrome." *American Journal of Psychiatry,* Vol. 131, 981-986, 1974.

Burgess, A.W. and Holmstrom, L.L. "Adaptive Strategies and Recovery from Rape." *American Journal of Psychiatry,* Vol. 136, 1278-1282, 1979.

Burgess, A. (ed.) *Rape and Sexual Assault*, Vol. I and II. New York: Garland Publishing Co., 1985 (vol. I); 1988 (vol. II).

Burkhart, B. R., and Stanton, A.L. "Sexual Agression in Acquaintance Relationships," in G. Russel (Ed.), *Violence in Intimate Relationships*. Englewood Cliffs, NJ: Spectrum, 1985.

Burt, M. and Katz, B. "Dimensions of Recovery from Rape: Focus on Growth Outcomes." *Journal of Interpersonal Violence*, Vol. 2, 57-82, 1987.

Costin, F. and Schwarz, N. "Beliefs about Rape and Women's Roles: A Four-nation Study." *Journal of Interpersonal Violence*, Vol. 2, 46-56, 1987.

Davis, L. *The Courage to Heal Workbook: For Women and Men Survivors of Child Sexual Abuse*. NY: Harper and Row, 1990.

Dull, R.T. and Giacopassi, D.J. "Demographic Correlates of Sexual and Dating Attitudes: A Study of Date Rape." *Criminal Justice and Behavior*, Vol. 14, No. 2, 175-193, 1987.

Ehrart, J.K. and Sandler, B. "Campus Gang Rape: Party Games." Association of American Colleges, *Project on the Status and Education of Women*, 1985.

Estrich, S. *Real Rape*. Cambridge, MA: Harvard University Press, 1987.

Flynn, C.P. "Sex Roles and Women's Response to Courtship Violence." *Journal of Family Violence*, Vol. 5, No. 1, 1990.

Giacopassi, D.J. and Wilkinson, K.R. "Rape and the Devalued Victim." *Law and Human Behavior*, Vol. 9, No. 4, 367-383, 1985.

Gordon, M.T. and Riger, S. *The Female Fear*. NY: The Free Press, 1989.

Gwartney-Gibbs, P.A., Stockard, J. and Bohmer, S. "Learning Courtship Aggression: The Influence of Parents, Peers, and Personal Experiences." *Family Relations: Journal of Applied Family & Child Studies*, Vol. 36, No. 3, 276-282, 1987.

Hagans, K. B. and Case, J. *When Your Child Has Been Molested: A Parent's Guide to Healing and Recovery*. Lexington, MA: Lexington Books, 1988.

Hall, E.R. "Adolescents' Perceptions of Sexual Assault." *Journal of Sex Education & Therapy*, Vol. 13, No. 1, 37-42, 1987.

Hazelwood, R.R. and Burgess, A.W. *Practical Aspects of Rape Investigation: A Multidisciplinary Approach*. NY: Elsevier, 1987.

Holstrom, L. and Burgess, A. *The Victim of Rape*. New Brunswick, NJ: Transaction Books, 1983.

Hunter, Mic. *Abused Boys: The Neglected Victims of Sexual Abuse*. Lexington, MA: Lexington Books, 1990.

Johnson, K. M. *If You Are Raped*. Holmes Beach, FL: Learning Publications, 1985.

Katz, J.H. *No Fairy Godmothers, No Magic Wands: The Healing Process After Rape*. CA: R & E Publishers, 1984.

Kelley, L. *Surviving Sexual Violence*. MN: University of Minnesota Press, 1988.

Koss, M. "The Hidden Rape Victim: Personality, Attitudinal, and Situational Characteristics." *Psychology of Women Quarterly*, Vol. 9, 193-212, 1985.

Koss, Mary P. and Harvey, Mary R. Edited by James Butcher. *The Rape Victim: Clinical and Community Approaches to Treatment*, Lexington, MA: The Stephen Greene Press, 1987.

Koss, M. P., Dinero, T. E., Seibel, C.A., and Cox, S.L. "Stranger and Acquaintance Rape: Are There Differences in the Victim's Experience?" *Psychology of Women Quarterly*, Vol. 12, pp. 1-23, 1988.

Koss, M. and Burkhart, B. "A Conceptual Analysis of Rape Victimization: Long-term Effects and Implications for Treatment." *Psychology of Women Quarterly*, Vol. 13, 27-40, 1989.

LaFree, G.D. *Rape and Criminal Justice: The Social Construction of Sexual Assault*. Belmont, CA: Wadsworth Publishing Co., 1989.

Larson, K. and Long, E. "Attitudes Toward Rape." *Journal of Sex Research*, Vol. 24, 299-304, 1988.

Ledray, L. *Recovering from Rape*. New York: Henry Holt and Co., 1986.

Lee, L. "Rape Prevention: Experiential Training for Men." *Journal of Counseling and Development*, Vol. 6, 100-101, 1987.

Levine, E.M. and Kanin, E.J. "Sexual Violence Among Dates and Acquaintances: Trends and the Implications for Marriage and Family." *Journal of Family Violence*, Vol. 2, No. 1, 55-65, 1987.

Levine-MacCombie, J. and Koss, M.P. "Acquaintance Rape: Effective Avoidance Strategies." *Psychology of Women Quarterly*, Vol. 10, No. 4, 311-319, 1986.

Lundberg-Love, P. and Geffner, R. "Date Rape: Prevalence, Risk Factors and a Proposed Model" in M. Pirog-Good and J. Stets, (Eds.), *Violence in Dating*. Praeger, 1988.

MacFarlane, K., and Waterman, J. (eds.), *Sexual Abuse of Young Children: Evaluation and Treatment*. New York: The Guilford Press, 1986.

Mayer, A. *Incest: A Treatment Manual for Therapy with Victims, Spouses, and Offenders*. Holmes Beach, FL: Learning Publications, Inc., 1983.

Mayer, A. *Sex Offenders: Approaches to Understanding and Management*. Holmes Beach, FL: Learning Publications, Inc., 1988.

McEvoy, A. and Erickson, E. *Youth and Exploitation*. Holmes Beach, FL: Learning Publications, Inc., 1990.

McEvoy, A. and Erickson, E. *Child Abuse and Neglect: A Guidebook for Educators and Community Leaders* (3rd ed.). Holmes Beach, FL: Learning Publications, Inc., 1991.

Muehlenhard, C.L. Freidman, D.E. and Thomas, C.M. "Is Date Rape Justifiable? The Effects of Dating Activity, Who Initiated, Who Paid, and Men's Attitudes Toward Women." *Psychology of Women Quarterly*, Vol. 9, No. 3, 297-310, 1985.

Muehlenhard, C. and Linton, M. "Date Rape and Sexual Aggression in Dating Situations: Incidence and Risk Factors." Association of American Colleges, *Project on the Status and Education of Women*, 1987.

Muehlenhard, C.L. "Misinterpreted Dating Behaviors and the Risk of Date Rape." *Journal of Social and Clinical Psychology*, Vol. 6, No. 1, 20-37, 1988.

Muehlenhard, C.L. and MacNaughton, J.S. "Women's Beliefs About Women who 'Lead Me On'." *Journal of Social and Clinical Psychology*, Vol. 7, No. 1, 65-79, 1988.

Muehlenhard, C., Julsonnet, S., and Flarity-White, L. "A Cognitive-Behavioral Program for Preventing Sexual Coercion." *Behavior Therapist*, Vol. 12, No. 9, 1989.

Murnen, S., Byrne, D. and Perot, A. "Coping with Unwanted Sexual Activity: Normative Responses, Situational Determinants, and Individual Differences." *Journal of Sex Research*, Vol. 26, 85-106, 1989.

O'Gorman-Hughes, J. and Sandler, B. "'Friends' Raping Friends: Could It Happen to You." Association of American Colleges, *Project on the Status and Education of Women*, 1987.

O'Gorman-Hughes, J. and Sandler, B. "Peer Harassment: Hassles for Women on Campus." Association of American Colleges, *Project on the Status and Education of Women*, 1988.

Parrot, A. *Coping with Date Rape and Acquaintance Rape*. New York: The Rosen Publishing Group, 1988.

Parrot, A. "Acquaintance Rape Among Adolescents: Identifying Risk Groups, and Intervention Strategies." *Journal of Social Work and Human Sexuality*, Vol. 8, 47-61, 1989.

Parrot, A. *Acquaintance Rape and Sexual Assault Prevention Training Manual* (4th ed.), New York: Cornell University, 1990.

Parrot, A. and Bechofer, L. (eds.), *Acquaintance Rape: The Hidden Crime*. New York: John Wiley and Sons, 1990.

Pirog-Good, M. and Stets, J. (eds.), *Violence in Dating Relationships: Emerging Social Issues*. New York: Praeger, 1989.

Reuterman, N.A. and Burcky, W. A. "Dating Violence in High School: A Profile of Victims." *Psychology: A Journal of Human Behavior*, Vol. 26, No. 4, 1989.

Roberts, C. *Women and Rape*. NY: Harvester Wheat Sheaf, 1989.

Rowland, J. *The Ultimate Violation*. NY: Doubleday and Company, Inc., 1985.

Ryan, K.M. "Rape and Seducation Scripts." *Psychology of Women Quarterly*, Vol. 12, No. 2, 237-245, 1988.

Schwendinger, J. R., & Schwendinger, H. *Rape and Inequality*. Beverly Hills, CA: Sage Publications, 1983.

Sgroi, S. *Handbook of Clinical Intervention in Child Sexual Abuse*. Lexington, MA: Lexington Books, 1982.

Tetreault, P.A. and Barnett, M.A. "Reactions to Stranger and Acquaintance Rape." *Psychology of Women Quarterly*, Vol. 11, 353-358, 1987.

Warshaw, R. *I Never Called It Rape: The Ms. Report on Recognizing, Fighting and Surviving Date and Acquaintance Rape*. New York: Harper & Row, 1988.

Yegidis, B.L. "Date Rape and Other Forced Sexual Encounters Among College Students." *Journal of Sex Education and Therapy*, Vol. 12, No. 2, 51-54, 1986.

Appendix C
Resources

National Organizations

National Assault Prevention Center
P. O. Box 02005
Columbus, OH 43202
(614) 291-2540

National Coalition Against Sexual Assault (NCASA)
2428 Ontario Road NW
Washington, DC 20009
(202) 483-7165

National Organization for Victim Assistance (NOVA)
1757 Park Road NW
Washington, DC 20010
(202) 393-6682

American Association for Counseling and Development
5999 Stevenson Avenue
Alexandria, VA 22304
(703) 823-9800

Alternatives to Fear
2811 E Madison, Suite 208
Seattle, WA 98112
(206) 328-5347

Clearinghouse on Child Abuse and Neglect Information
P. O. Box 1182
Washington, DC 20013
(703) 821-2086

National Child Abuse Hotline/Childhelp, USA
P. O. Box 630
Hollywood, CA 90028
(800) 422-4453 (hotline)
(213) 465-4016

National Resource Center on Child Sexual Abuse
11141 Georgia Ave, Suite 310
Wheaton, MD 20902
(301) 949-5000
(800) 543-7006 (for professionals)

Institute for the Study of Sexual Assault
403 Asbury Street
San Francisco, CA 94116
(415) 861-2048

National Committee for Prevention of Child Abuse
332 S. Michigan Avenue
Suite 1600
Chicago, IL 60604
(312) 663-3520

National Clearinghouse on Marital and Date Rape
2325 Oak Street
Berkeley, CA 94708
(415) 548-1770

Men Stopping Rape
839 Williamson St. #3
Madison, WI 53703

National Organization for Victim Assistance
Dept. P, 717 "D" Street NW
Washington, DC 20004
(202) 393-6682

In Canada write to:

Victims of Violence
Victims Rights Advocates
Box 86
Ajax, Ontario, L1S 3C2
(416) 683-2639

Canadian Child Welfare Association
2211 Riverside Drive
Ottawa, Ontario, K1H 7X5
(613) 738-0697

National Victims Resource Centre
Ministry of the Solicitor General
340 Laurier Avenue West
Ottawa, Ontario, K1A 0P8
(613) 990-2757 (National Capital Region)
1-800-267-0464 (from elsewhere in Canada)

Local Organizations

There are many ways to locate such resources in your
community:

1. Check the telephone directory.

2. Call your local hospital or police department.

3. Check with other human service agencies such as
   Child Guidance, Child Protective Services, or the

YWCA. If there are rape crisis services in your area, they will be aware of them.

4. In the event all the above attempts fail, contact one of the national organizations listed above. Staff members will be able to help you find the closest possible rape crisis service in your area.